Chaffle Mania

75 No Sugar, No Flour Chaffle Recipes for Weight Loss

Nicole De Falcis

Any recipe that was seen on social media and made no sugar, no flour, and/or less cheese compliant by Nicole will have an asterisk next to the recipe title. Otherwise, the recipes are 100% her creation.

Printed in the United States of America

ISBN 978-0-578-85662-9

To my mom and dad,

who are good for my soul.

I am beyond grateful for you.

CONTENTS

Lunch

Lunch/Dinner

Introduction

Hello, everyone! I'm Nicole De Falcis!

As a former manager and trainer for a weight loss company, I know what foods I should eat and how to cook healthy. However, somehow with the busyness of life and working too many hours, I lost my way by gaining and losing the same weight over the last 15 years! Knowing how does not always translate into doing, am I right?

Fast forward to January 2020: I decided on a whim to stop eating all sugar and grains. I had never read anything about this way of eating and just did what felt right for my body. Then during the COVID-19 lockdown, I started eating all the food I had eliminated for 2 ½ months and gained back the weight I had lost. I then realized I had to make a permanent and sustainable lifestyle plan!

Shortly after, I heard of a healthy way of eating in which I would eliminate sugar and flour, yet still eat healthy grains. On August 3, 2020, I began a no sugar, no flour *lifestyle*. I finally realized that I needed a sustainable weight loss option to keep the weight off. My husband joined me about a month later, which made it more fun.

The best things I've discovered during this weight loss journey are that I never feel too hungry, I love the food, I have more energy, my much smaller clothes are fitting, and I am feeling a new purpose in life. I am thoroughly enjoying using and creating new recipes and the camaraderie from no sugar, no flour FACEBOOK® groups.

I made my first Chaffle a few days before New Year's Eve 2020 and was hooked. In January 2021, I started creating Chaffles and posting pics and recipes. Soon, others on the no sugar, no flour Facebook groups quickly jumped on board. Many dubbed me the *"Chaffle Queen"* and encouraged me to write a Chaffle cookbook.

May you find health and joy from this no sugar, no flour lifestyle and have loads of fun making Chaffles!

Forward

Are you ready to have some fun with your food? Bonus question: are you ready to lose some weight too? You are? Then welcome to *Chaffle Mania*. This inaugural, ground-breaking publication from my dear friend, Nicole De Falcis, is packed with amazing no sugar, no flour Chaffle recipes that are not only healthy, but also extremely delicious. Get ready for recipes that have revamped your childhood comfort meals, your favorite breakfast, and recreated a burger like no other. Seriously, you won't be missing the sugar and the flour at all and you'll be amazed at how much flavor you experience.

Why no sugar, no flour? Numerous studies (and personal testimonies) have shown that these two substances are the major culprit in weight gain and loss of appetite control. The biological effects sugar and flour have on our body are well documented. These detrimental effects include hormonal imbalances, inflammation, brain fog, sluggish metabolism, digestive issues, and in extreme cases diabetes and cardiovascular disease. If that information isn't convincing enough for you to severely reduce or eliminate your sugar and flour intake, perhaps this will. For many of us, sugar and flour are extremely addicting. It turns out that both substances trigger the same neurological response in our brain as cocaine, which explains why we crave that certain sweet and why we can't stop at "just one bite". Ask any nutritionist, dietician, or doctor - eliminating sugar and flour will change more than just your appearance, it will improve your health.

A while ago, Nicole and I decided it's time to get healthy for good, and this time it's going to be something that is tasty *and* sustainable. We decided to eliminate all processed sugar and flour from our diet. Your first response to adopting a no sugar, no flour, lifestyle may be, "okay, that sounds great but now I need to get ready for a life of tasteless food that I will not look forward to eating." I am here to testify and let you know that statement is the farthest thing from the truth. I honestly have never had such a balanced, filling, and nutritious way of eating before. My meals are filled with fresh fruits and vegetables, healthy grains and fats, and filling proteins. Nicole has been the creative genius behind many of my favorite recipes. She is one of the most inventive and dedicated people I know. When she puts her mind to something, watch out, because it is going to be amazing. Case in point, this lovely collection of Chaffle recipes. Many of these recipes have been tried, tested, and praised by those following "Nicole's Weight Loss Eating" and other no sugar, no flour Facebook groups. Indeed, these recipes have been lovingly curated for maximum flavor and weight loss benefits to boot!

You know the saying "you eat with your eyes first"? It's true, take a look at the pictures of these delicious Chaffles. Are they not appetizing? Look at the Cherry Bliss Chaffles on page 76. Is this not absolutely delightful to look at? I promise you all your senses will enjoy this Chaffle experience. The smell that will travel throughout your house when you make the Pecan Butter Bananas Foster Chaffles on page 98 will cause family and neighbors to pop their heads in and ask "what's cookin'?". The crispy exterior and delightfully crunchy interior of the Corn Fritters Chaffles on page 142 makes for a fully enjoyable experience that satisfies every texture craving. And lastly, the taste! The taste will leave you wanting nothing. You will be happy, satisfied, fulfilled. The whole process of prepping, mixing, cooking, assembly, and eating will fill you with pride because you just made a delectable and healthy meal.

Whether you're on the no sugar, no flour bandwagon or just love the thought of making a fun meal in a waffle maker, I'm so glad you're here. Enjoy!

Christina Swan, Ph.D.

Nicole’s Chaffle Tips

1. I encourage you to buy a quality 4″ mini waffle maker. I use the Mini Waffle Maker by DASH®. In each recipe I will mention “mini waffle maker” and not the product name. Please see earlier disclaimer.
Note: I have quite a few recipes that work using a large waffle maker and this is indicated underneath the recipe title.
2. If you decide to buy a mini waffle maker that makes 4 waffles at a time, I use the Multi Mini Waffle Maker by DASH® that has four 4″ *circles*.
3. Preheat your mini waffle maker and make sure and put a plate underneath to catch all the mess from oil spray. I mention this on almost every recipe. This helps me since I am a messy cook.
4. I recommend coconut oil spray for sweet Chaffles and olive, or avocado oil spray for savory Chaffles.
5. Most of my recipes call for spraying just the top of the mini waffle maker since you put cheese on the bottom before adding the mix. This helps Chaffles not to stick and makes them crispy.
6. Chaffles would be crispier with cheese on the bottom AND the top of the mini waffle maker, but that adds too much cheese to most of the recipes. Add more cheese if you feel like that is okay for you.
7. Always place Chaffle, with crispy side face down on the plate and put topping on the softer side.
8. Once you have made many Chaffles and know what sticks and what doesn’t, you can get to the point that you might not add any oil spray at all if you are using a good quality mini waffle maker.
9. The worst culprits for sticking are the following in no specific order: pumpkin, carrots, cauliflower rice, spinach, pineapple, spaghetti squash, zucchini, and chickpeas. My

advice would be to refrain from any peeking, and especially on these items. I call these the ***sticky EIGHT***!

10. I rarely beat the large egg ahead of time for Chaffles. I just throw ingredients all in a bowl and mix until the egg is beaten. I do mash the banana first, most of the time.

11. If a Chaffle recipe does not have BOTH egg AND cheese, then it is not actually a Chaffle! I have a small category at the end of my book for a few in that category. Yummy, but not really Chaffles.

12. I cook all my Chaffles for 3 minutes or longer. I have never had one burn in my mini waffle maker, but I would not cook a Chaffle longer than 5 minutes.

13. To make Chaffles even crispier, you may place them 1-2 minutes on a wire cooling rack. Some of my recipes instruct to do this and others don't. Why? Because I prefer my Chaffles warmer, so I often skip the wire cooling rack.

14. I use large eggs in almost all of my recipes. The large eggs from the store weigh 2 oz which works well for a Chaffle recipe. My recipes indicate which size egg to use.

15. I always use garlic granules instead of garlic powder, even if garlic powder is listed. Garlic granules give more flavor. Likewise for onion granules.

16. My all-time favorite seasoning is HERBAMARE® Herbed Sea Salt by A. Vogel. I discovered it many years ago when my sister-in-law, Marina, brought it to us from Switzerland. Fun Fact: It was developed in Switzerland and is now made in Colmar, France. You can find it at health food stores or buy online. I use it in any recipe that calls for "*seasoned* sea salt".

17. I do NOT recommend using Quick Oats in any of my recipes. They break down too easily and change the texture. It is best to use Rolled Oats, uncooked.

18. I use the word *sprinkles* for the cheese that you will sprinkle on the bottom of the mini waffle maker before adding the mix.

19. Mozzarella cheese is healthier than most cheeses and takes on the flavor of the other food easily, therefore I use it in most of my recipes. However, shredded parmesan cheese

is great because it weighs less than most cheese, so you get more cheese sprinkles.

20. It is preferable to bake potatoes for my recipes, rather than boil them so they will not have as much moisture.
21. Sadly, Chaffles don't get crispy using vegan cheese. I have tried at least 6 brands and they don't even resemble the Chaffles with real cheese.
22. You will discover that I often use bananas as a sweetener in the mix and/or the topping. When I use banana as a sweetener, it is indicated. It is best to use very ripe bananas.
23. Nicole's Basic Chaffle works very well made in bulk, refrigerated (or frozen) and used for sandwiches. I use a canister that I bought online to store mine in the fridge.
24. Mexican style cheese blend makes Chaffles crispier, but I have not been able to find it in bulk, so I don't use it much. Other finely shredded cheeses work very well, but they are also more expensive.
25. The possibilities are endless with Chaffles! Have fun!

For a lunch or dinner sandwich, you can count the cheese as a full fat serving and add 2 oz of protein in the sandwich.

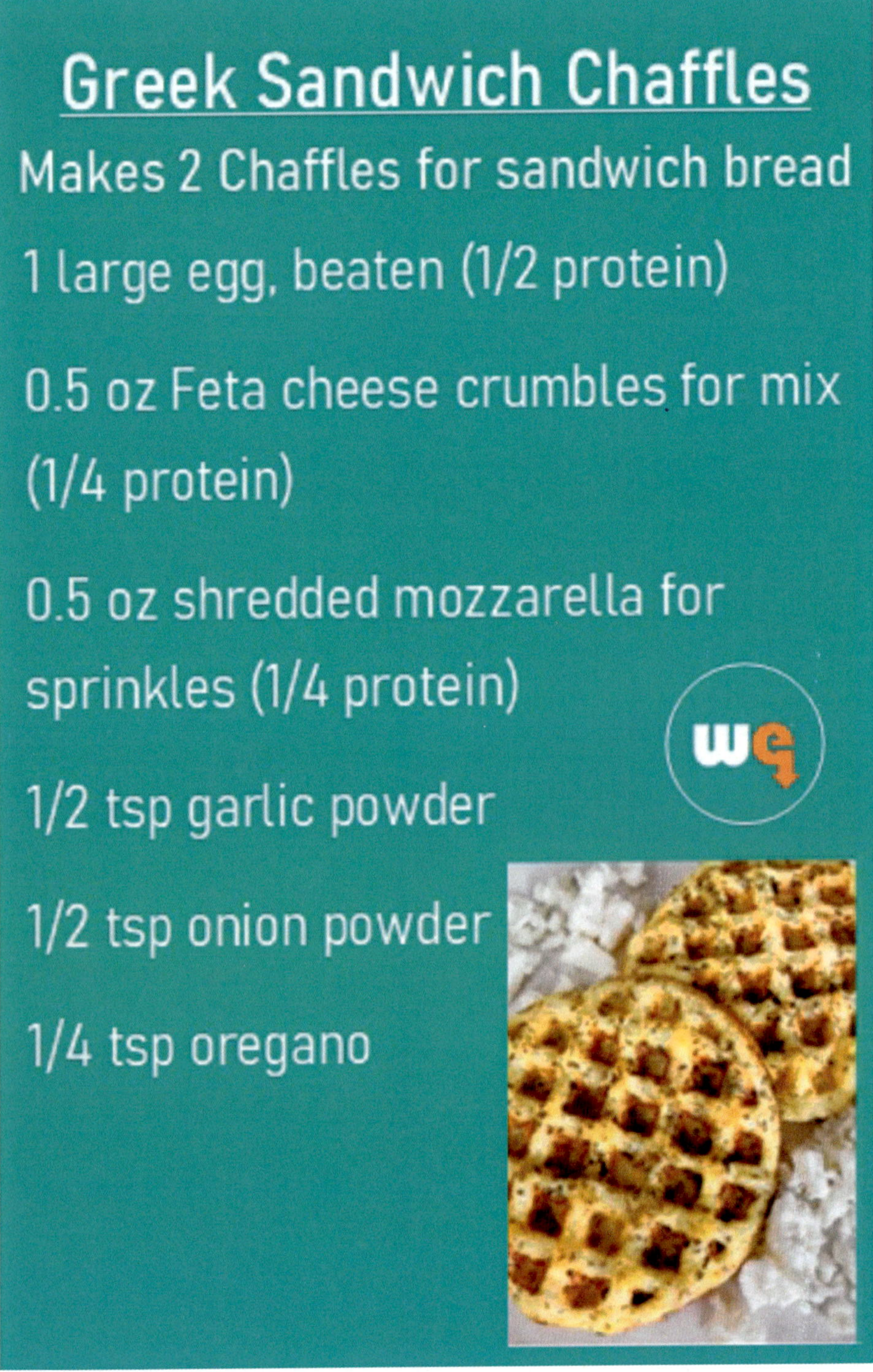

Greek Sandwich Chaffles

Makes 2 Chaffles for sandwich bread

1 large egg, beaten (1/2 protein)

0.5 oz Feta cheese crumbles for mix (1/4 protein)

0.5 oz shredded mozzarella for sprinkles (1/4 protein)

1/2 tsp garlic powder

1/2 tsp onion powder

1/4 tsp oregano

For a lunch or dinner sandwich, you can count the cheese as a full fat serving and add 2 oz of protein in the sandwich.

BREAKFAST

Banana Nut Bread Chaffles

Makes 3 breakfast Chaffles in mini waffle maker. Provides complete breakfast grain, complete protein, and complete fruit. This recipe can be made in a large waffle maker.

Ingredients for Chaffles:

- 1 large egg, beaten (1/2 protein)
- 1 oz uncooked oats (full grain)
- 3 oz banana, mashed
- 0.5 oz pecan pieces (1/4 protein). Weigh *before* putting into mix.
- 1/4 tsp cinnamon
- 1 tsp vanilla extract
- 1 tsp maple extract

Ingredients to Reserve:

- 0.5 oz mozzarella cheese, shredded (1/4 protein), for sprinkles
- oil spray

Ingredients for Topping:

- 3 oz blueberries heated in microwave. I used frozen, wild blueberries.
- 1/4 tsp maple extract, added to blueberries

Instructions:

1. Heat mini waffle maker. Make sure you place a plate underneath to catch mess.
2. Mash banana and add other ingredients. Mix well and divide into thirds.
3. Spray waffle maker on top side. Put sprinkles of mozzarella at bottom of waffle maker to help make it crispy. Cook 1/3 of Chaffle mix. Remove Chaffle and follow the same instructions for the second and third Chaffles. Do NOT peek! Wait until all steam is gone.
4. I cooked each Chaffle for 3 minutes. This is a good time to make the topping.
5. Microwave the blueberries until soft and add maple extract.
6. Place the crispy side face down onto plate and stack the Chaffles. Pour Topping, with juice, onto stack of Chaffles.

Hash Brown Casserole Chaffles

Makes 3 breakfast Chaffles in mini waffle maker. Provides complete grain, complete protein, 1 oz veggie (counted as fruit). This recipe can be made in a large waffle maker.

Ingredients for Chaffles:

- 1 large egg, beaten (1/2 protein)
- 4 oz frozen hash browns (shredded potatoes) (full grain)
- 0.5 oz onions, chopped
- 0.5 oz bell pepper, chopped
- 0.5 oz cheddar cheese, shredded (1/4 protein)
- 1/2 tsp chili garlic CHOLULA® HOT SAUCE (or TABASCO®)
- 1/2 tsp onion powder
- 1/2 tsp garlic powder
- 1/8 tsp seasoned sea salt

Ingredients to Reserve:

- 0.5 oz cheddar cheese, shredded (1/4 protein), for sprinkles
- oil spray

Instructions:

1. Defrost hash browns. Press dry with paper towel. No need to squeeze out water with nut milk bag.
2. Heat mini waffle maker. Make sure you place a plate underneath to catch mess.
3. Chop veggies into small pieces. Mix all Chaffle ingredients.
4. Spray waffle maker on top side. Put sprinkles of cheddar at bottom of waffle maker to help make it crispy. Cook 1/3 of Chaffle mix. Remove Chaffle and follow the same instructions for the second and third Chaffles. Do NOT peek! Wait until all steam is gone.
5. Cook each Chaffle for 4 minutes, or longer, if you want it crispier. As an option, you could pre-cook your hash browns.

Note: Serve with 5 oz fruit.

Berries-n-Cream Chaffles

Makes 3 breakfast Chaffles in mini waffle maker. Provides complete grain, complete protein, and complete fruit. This recipe can be made in a large waffle maker.

Ingredients for Chaffles:

- 1 large egg, beaten (1/2 protein)
- 1 oz uncooked oats (full grain)
- 2 oz frozen mixed berries (strawberries, blueberries, & raspberries) defrosted in microwave and drained of ALL juice
- 1.5 oz banana, mashed (used as a sweetener)
- 0.25 oz parmesan cheese, fresh, shredded (1/8 protein),
- 1/2 tsp maple extract
- 1 tsp vanilla extract
- 1/2 tsp cinnamon

Ingredients to Reserve:

- 0.25 oz parmesan cheese, fresh, shredded (1/8 protein), for sprinkles
- oil spray

Ingredients for Topping:

- 1 oz ricotta cheese (1/4 protein)
- 0.5 oz banana, mashed (used as a sweetener)
- 2 oz frozen mixed berries heated in microwave, Reserve juice!
- dash vanilla extract

Instructions:

1. Heat mini waffle maker. Make sure you place a plate underneath to catch mess.
2. Mash banana. Defrost mixed berries and drain all juice. Add other Chaffle ingredients. Mix well and envision it divided into thirds. It will be too liquid to divide.
3. Spray waffle maker on top side. Put sprinkles of parmesan at bottom of waffle maker to help make it crispy. Cook 1/3 of Chaffle mix. Remove Chaffle and follow the same instructions for the second and third Chaffles. Do NOT peek! Wait until all steam is gone.
4. I cooked each Chaffle for 3 minutes. This is a good time to make the topping. Mash banana. Microwave the frozen berries until soft. Reserve the juice from berries. Add ricotta to banana and berries with juice and gently mix. Do not mash! You should get a pretty purple color.
5. Place the crispy side face down onto plate and put topping on the softer side. Chaffles could be layered with topping on each layer.

Cuban Rice & Beans Chaffles

Makes 3 breakfast Chaffles in mini waffle maker. Provides complete protein and complete grain. Would work in a large waffle maker.

Ingredients for Chaffles:

- 1 large egg, beaten (1/2 protein)
- 4 oz precooked rice (full grain)
- 1.5 oz precooked black beans, well-drained (1/4 protein)
- 1/2 tsp onion powder
- 1/2 tsp garlic powder
- 1/2 tsp cumin
- 1/4 tsp oregano
- 1 tsp lime juice
- 1/4 tsp sea salt

Ingredients to Reserve:

- 0.5 oz Swiss or mozzarella cheese, shredded (1/4 protein), for sprinkles
- oil spray

Ingredient for Topping:

- 1 TBSP green onion, chopped (free condiment)

Instructions:

1. Heat mini waffle maker. Make sure you place a plate underneath to catch mess.
2. Mix all Chaffle ingredients.
3. Spray waffle maker on top side. Put sprinkles of Swiss cheese at bottom of waffle maker to help make it crispy. Cook 1/3 of Chaffle mix. Remove Chaffle and follow the same instructions for the second and third Chaffles. Do NOT peek! Wait until all steam is gone.
4. Cook each Chaffle for 4 minutes, or longer, if you want it crispier.

Note: Serve with 6 oz fruit. Sautéed or air fried banana would work well!

Peach Chaffles

Makes 3 breakfast Chaffles in mini waffle maker. Provides complete protein, complete grain, and complete fruit. A large waffle maker would work.

Ingredients for Chaffles:

- 1 large egg, beaten (1/2 protein)
- 1 oz uncooked oats (full grain)
- 2 oz peaches, small cut and patted dry with a paper towel
- 1 oz banana, mashed (used as a sweetener)
- 1/2 tsp cinnamon
- 1 tsp vanilla extract
- 1/2 tsp maple extract
- 1/8 tsp nutmeg

Ingredients to Reserve:

- 0.5 oz mozzarella cheese, shredded (1/4 protein), for sprinkles
- oil spray

Ingredients for Topping:

- 3 oz sliced peaches
- 1 oz cottage cheese (1/4 protein)

Instructions:

1. Cut peaches, drain, and pat dry with a paper towel.
2. Heat mini waffle maker. Make sure you place a plate underneath to catch mess.
3. Mash banana and add other Chaffle ingredients. Mix well and divide into thirds.
4. Spray mini waffle maker on top side. Put sprinkles of mozzarella at bottom of waffle maker to help make it crispy. Cook 1/3 of Chaffle mix. Remove Chaffle and follow the same instructions for the second and third Chaffles. Do NOT peek! Wait until all steam is gone.
5. I cooked each Chaffle for 3 minutes. This is a good time to slice the peaches and weigh the cottage cheese for the topping.
6. Place the crispy side face down onto plate and put topping on the softer side.

I'd been wondering how grits would taste in a Chaffle, then I had an idea to make a Chaffle out of it and add seasoning with BUTTER EXTRACT. It tastes like cornbread! So yummy!! I did a search and couldn't find anything like this, yet it's so simple, so I was pleasantly surprised. Notice the Chaffle in front looks crispier. I sprinkled cheese on the mini waffle maker before adding the mix and it's much better for this recipe, and for most of them!

Cornbread Chaffles

Makes 2 breakfast Chaffles in mini waffle maker. Provides complete protein and grain.

Ingredients for Chaffles:

- 4 oz precooked instant grits (1 grain)
- 1 large egg, beaten (1/2 protein)
- 0.5 oz cheddar cheese, shredded (1/4 protein)
- 1 1/4 tsp butter extract
- 1/4 tsp garlic powder
- 1/4 tsp onion powder
- 1/2 tsp baking powder
- 1/8 tsp seasoned sea salt

Ingredients to Reserve:

- 0.5 oz cheddar cheese, shredded (1/4 protein), for sprinkles
- oil spray

Instructions:

1. Cook instant corn grits, adding minimal boiling water. I used plain instant grits: 1 3/4 oz dry instant grits equal 4 oz cooked, or almost two packets. Optional: You could use raw polenta, cooked.
2. Heat mini waffle maker. Place a plate underneath to catch the mess.
3. Mix Chaffle ingredients.
4. Spray top of waffle maker with oil. Put sprinkles of cheese on bottom of waffle maker. Add half the mix. Cook until steam is gone. Follow the same instructions for the second Chaffle.
5. Cook for 3 minutes. Cook longer to make it crispier.
6. Cool for 1-2 minutes on a wire cooling rack.

Note: Serve with 6 oz fruit.

In many parts of the south in the US, it's a tradition to eat black-eyed peas on New Year's Day to bring luck, and cabbage, or another green, to bring wealth. I've always made a big pot of fresh black-eyed peas for New Year's Day and I had some leftover. I also had some leftover rice. Knowing rice and beans go very well together gave me this idea, coupled with a family New Year's Day tradition.

Southern Belle Chaffles

Makes 2 breakfast Chaffles in mini waffle maker. Provides complete protein and grain.

Ingredients for Chaffles:

- 4 oz precooked rice (full grain)

Note: I use Arborio rice (risotto style rice) in many of my recipes, not all, because I like the taste and texture better in Chaffles.

- 1 large egg, beaten (1/2 protein)
- 1.5 oz precooked black-eyed peas (1/4 protein)
- 1/4 tsp garlic powder
- 1/4 tsp onion powder
- 1/8 tsp seasoned sea salt

Ingredients to Reserve:

- 0.5 oz cheddar cheese, shredded (1/4 protein), for sprinkles
- oil spray

Instructions:

1. Heat mini waffle maker. Place a plate underneath to catch the mess.
2. Mix all Chaffle ingredients.
3. Spray top of waffle maker. Sprinkle half of cheese on bottom of waffle maker. Add half of the mix. Cook until steam is gone. Do not peek! Continue with the same instructions for the second Chaffle.
4. Cook for 4 minutes.
5. Cool for 1-2 minutes on a wire cooling rack, so it's crispier.

Notes:

1. My black-eyed peas had lots of seasoning added when I cooked them from fresh, so you might want to add 1/2 tsp of garlic and onion powders if yours are not very seasoned, or if you are using canned black-eyed peas.
2. Do NOT peek! This Chaffle is not forgiving with peeking. Cook it a little longer after steam is gone.
3. Serve with 6 oz fruit.

Optional: Use other beans instead and *change seasonings* accordingly:

*Use black beans to make a Cuban style Chaffle.

*Use pinto beans to make a Mexican style Chaffle.

*Use white beans to make an Italian style Chaffle.

My husband, Nino, was born and raised in Switzerland. I never had rhubarb until a few years ago and I could understand why he likes it so much. I changed this recipe several times until it got the Swiss stamp of approval. He loves the tartness of it, just like they make it in Switzerland.

Swiss Tarte à la Rhubarbe Chaffles

Makes 3 breakfast Chaffles in mini waffle maker. Provides complete grain, complete protein, and complete fruit. This recipe would work in a large waffle maker.

Ingredients for Chaffles:

- 1 large egg, beaten (1/2 protein)
- 2.5 oz frozen rhubarb, heated in microwave and mashed
- 1 oz banana, mashed (used as a sweetener)
- 1 oz uncooked oats (full grain)
- 1/2 tsp cinnamon
- 1 tsp vanilla extract

Ingredients to Reserve:

- 0.5 oz mozzarella cheese, shredded (1/4 protein), for sprinkles
- oil spray

Ingredients for Topping:

- 1 oz ricotta cheese (1/4 protein)
- 2 oz frozen rhubarb, heated in microwave and mashed
- 0.5 banana, mashed (used as a sweetener)
- dash of vanilla extract

Instructions:

1. Heat mini waffle maker. Make sure you place a plate underneath to catch mess.
2. Defrost rhubarb in microwave. Mash banana and add other Chaffle ingredients. Mix well and divide into thirds.
3. Spray waffle maker on top. Put sprinkles of mozzarella at bottom of waffle maker to help make it crispy. Cook 1/3 of Chaffle mix. Remove Chaffle and follow the same instructions for the second and third Chaffles. Do NOT peek! Wait until all steam is gone.
4. Make topping while Chaffles are cooking. Defrost and mash rhubarb, then add banana and mash. Add ricotta and vanilla and mix well. Let Chaffles cool for 1-2 minutes before adding topping. Spread topping on Chaffles and layer them.

Note: The Swiss eat their rhubarb pie very tarte. It's delicious! However, if you prefer it less tarte you could switch out some of the rhubarb for more banana, or for strawberry.

Shrimp & Grits Chaffles

Makes 3 breakfast Chaffles in mini waffle maker. Provides complete grain and complete protein. Would work in a large waffle maker.

Ingredients for Chaffles:

- 1 large egg, beaten (1/2 protein)
- 4 oz precooked instant grits (full grain) Cook instant corn grits, adding minimal boiling water.
- 1 oz shrimp, cooked and cut into small pieces. (1/4 protein) Use about 4 medium shrimp.
- 0.25 oz cheddar, shredded (1/8 protein)
- 1/4 tsp seasoned sea salt
- 1/2 tsp onion powder
- 1/2 tsp garlic powder
- 1/2 tsp butter extract

Ingredients to Reserve:

- 0.25 oz cheddar cheese, shredded (1/8 protein), for sprinkles. Not much for cheese sprinkles, so make sure and cool for 1-2 minutes.
- oil spray

Ingredient for Topping:

- 1 TBSP green onion, chopped (free condiment)

Instructions:

1. For this recipe I use frozen, peeled, and deveined raw shrimp. That way I have it handy when needed. To cook the shrimp, spray a pan with oil and add seasonings of choice. Let cool before cutting into small pieces.
2. Heat mini waffle maker. Make sure you place a plate underneath to catch mess.
3. Mix all Chaffle ingredients together, including shrimp. Divide into thirds.
4. Spray mini waffle maker on top side. Put sprinkles of cheddar at bottom of waffle maker to help make it crispy. Cook 1/3 of Chaffle mix. Remove Chaffle and follow the same instructions for the second and third Chaffles. Do NOT peek! Wait until all steam is gone.
5. Cook each Chaffle for 4 minutes, or longer, if you want it crispier. Cool them 1-2 minutes on a wire cooling rack.
6. Top with green onions.

Note: Serve with 6 oz fruit.

Key Lime Pie Chaffles

Makes 2 breakfast Chaffles in mini waffle maker. Provides complete protein and complete grain.

Ingredients for Chaffles:

- 1 large egg, beaten (1/2 protein)
- 1.5 oz banana, mashed (used as a sweetener)
- 1 oz uncooked oats (full grain)
- 1/2 tsp vanilla extract
- 1 tsp Key lime extract
- zest of two Key limes
- juice of one Key lime

Ingredients to Reserve:

- 0.5 oz mozzarella cheese, shredded (1/4 protein), for sprinkles
- oil spray

Ingredients for Topping:

- 1 oz ricotta cheese (1/4 protein)
- 1 oz mashed banana (used as a sweetener)
- 1/2 tsp Key lime extract
- zest of half a Key lime

Instructions:

1. Heat mini waffle maker. Make sure you place a plate underneath to catch mess.
2. Mix Chaffle ingredients and divide in half.
3. Spray mini waffle maker on BOTH sides for this recipe. Put sprinkles of mozzarella at bottom of waffle maker to help make it crispy. Cook 1/2 of Chaffle mix. Remove Chaffle and follow the same instructions for the second Chaffle. Do NOT peek! Wait until all steam is gone.
4. I cooked each Chaffle for 4 minutes. This is a good time to make the topping.
5. Once the Chaffles have cooled for 1-2 minutes, place topping on one Chaffle and put 2nd Chaffle on top layering the pie. Put the remainder of the topping on the top.

Note: Serve with 3.5 oz fruit.

Wow! Just wow! Just out of this world delicious! Can you tell I miss traveling? Now we can bring traveling to our kitchens while not eating sugar and flour. These are for breakfast and the perfect pairing with small, frozen pieces of passion fruit. It seriously seemed like I was eating in a restaurant!

Japanese Rice Chaffles

Makes 3 breakfast Chaffles in mini waffle maker. Provides full protein and full grain. Would work in a large waffle iron.

Ingredients for Chaffles:

- 4 oz precooked sushi rice, or you can use Arborio risotto style rice. (Full grain)
- 1 large egg, beaten (1/2 protein)
- 0.5 oz mozzarella cheese, shredded (1/4 protein)
- 3 small, roasted seaweed sheets (Nori)- I counted this as a free condiment, because it weighed nothing in ounces or in grams!
- 1/4 tsp onion powder
- 1/4 tsp garlic powder
- 1/4 tsp plain sea salt
- 1/2 tsp shiitake mushroom powder (or porcini mushroom powder if you have that instead)

Ingredients to Reserve:

- 0.5 oz mozzarella cheese, shredded (1/4 protein), for sprinkles
- oil spray

Instructions:

1. Heat mini waffle maker. Use a plate underneath to help catch the mess.
2. Mix Chaffle ingredients. Crumble seaweed sheets into the mix.
3. Divide mix into thirds.
4. Spray top of waffler maker with oil. Put a FEW sprinkles of mozzarella cheese onto bottom of waffle maker, cover with 1/3 mix and cook. Wait until all steam is gone. The longer you cook it, the crispier it gets, but putting sprinkles of cheese first will make it crispier too. Repeat same instructions for second and third Chaffles.

Note: For a complete breakfast add 6 oz fruit. I had 6 oz frozen chunks of passion fruit and that was a fabulous combo!

Savory Quinoa & Beets Breakfast Chaffles

Makes 3 "thick" breakfast Chaffles in mini waffle maker. Provides complete protein, complete grain, and 3 oz fruit. Would work in a large waffle maker.

Ingredients for Chaffles:

- 1 large egg, beaten (1/2 protein)
- 4 oz precooked quinoa (full grain)
- 3 oz precooked beets, cut into small pieces (1/2 fruit)
- 0.5 oz crumbled Feta cheese (1/4 protein)
- 1/2 tsp garlic powder
- 1/2 tsp onion powder
- no salt

Ingredients to Reserve:

- 0.5 oz mozzarella cheese, shredded, (1/4 protein), for sprinkles
- oil spray

Instructions:

1. Heat mini waffle maker. Make sure you place a plate underneath to catch mess.
2. Chop precooked beets into small pieces. Mix all Chaffle ingredients.
3. Spray waffle maker on top side. Put sprinkles of mozzarella at bottom of waffle maker to help make it crispy. Cook 1/3 of Chaffle mix. Remove Chaffle and follow the same instructions for the second and third Chaffles. Do NOT peek! Wait until all steam is gone.
4. Cook each Chaffle for 4 minutes, or longer, if you want it crispier.

Note: Serve with 3 oz fruit.

Blueberry Lemon Chaffles

Makes 2 breakfast Chaffles in mini waffle maker. Provides complete protein, complete grain, and complete fruit.

Ingredients for Chaffles:

- 1 egg, beaten (1/2 protein)
- 1 oz uncooked oats (full grain)
- 2 oz banana, mashed (used as a sweetener)
- 2 oz defrosted blueberries, strained of juice (don't add the juice to the mix)
- 0.5 oz mozzarella cheese, shredded (1/4 protein)
- 1 tsp lemon zest (about 1 large lemon)
- 1 tsp lemon extract
- 1/2 tsp vanilla extract
- 1/2 tsp cinnamon

Ingredients to Reserve:

- 0.5 oz mozzarella cheese, shredded (1/4 protein), for sprinkles
- oil spray

Ingredients for Topping:

- 2 oz heated blueberries, with juice
- 1 TBSP fresh lemon juice

Instructions:

1. Heat mini waffle maker. Make sure you place a plate underneath to catch mess.
2. Mix Chaffle ingredients well and divide in half.
3. Spray waffle maker on top side. Put sprinkles of mozzarella at bottom of waffle maker to help make it crispy. Cook 1/2 of Chaffle mix. Remove Chaffle and follow the same instructions for the second Chaffle. Do NOT peek! Wait until all steam is gone.
4. While second Chaffle is cooking, prepare the topping.
5. Place crispy side down on plate and serve with topping.

Sweet Potato Casserole Chaffles

Makes 3 breakfast Chaffles in mini waffle maker. Provides complete grain, complete protein, and 2.5 oz fruit. This recipe can be made in a large waffle maker.

Ingredients for Chaffles:

- 1 large egg, beaten (1/2 protein)
- 4 oz sweet potato, precooked, peeled, & mashed (full grain)
- 1.5 oz banana, mashed (used as a sweetener)
- 0.25 oz pecan pieces (1/8 protein) Weigh before adding to mix.
- 1/2 tsp cinnamon
- 1/2 tsp butter extract
- 1 tsp vanilla extract
- dash sea salt

Ingredients to Reserve:

- 0.25 oz mozzarella cheese, shredded (1/8 protein), for sprinkles
- oil spray

Ingredients for Topping:

- 1 oz ricotta cheese (1/4 protein)
- 1 oz banana, mashed (used as a sweetener)

Instructions:

1. Heat mini waffle maker. Make sure you place a plate underneath to catch mess.
2. Mix Chaffle ingredients and divide into thirds.
3. Spray waffle maker on top side. Put sprinkles of mozzarella at bottom of waffle maker to help make it crispy. Cook 1/3 of Chaffle mix. Remove Chaffle and follow the same instructions for the second and third Chaffles. Do NOT peek! Wait until all steam is gone. Sweet potato tends to stick.
4. While third Chaffle is cooking, make the topping. You may either layer the Chaffles and put topping on each layer or serve separately as in the photo.

Note: Serve with 3.5 oz fruit.

Strawberry Shortcake Chaffles

Makes 3 breakfast Chaffles in mini waffle maker. Provides complete grain, complete protein, and complete fruit. This recipe can be made in a large waffle maker.

Ingredients for Chaffles:

- 1 large egg, beaten (1/2 protein)
- 1 oz uncooked oats (full grain)
- 2.5 oz fresh strawberries, sliced
- 1 oz banana, mashed (used as a sweetener)
- 1 tsp strawberry extract
- 1 tsp vanilla extract
- 1/4 tsp cinnamon
- 1/8 tsp baking powder

Ingredients to Reserve:

- 0.5 oz mozzarella cheese, shredded, (1/4 protein), for sprinkles
- oil spray

Ingredients for Topping:

- 2 oz strawberries, heated in microwave
- 1 oz ricotta cheese (1/4 protein)
- 0.5 oz banana, mashed (used as a sweetener)

Instructions:

1. Heat mini waffle maker. Make sure you place a plate underneath to catch mess.
2. Mix Chaffle ingredients and divide into thirds.
3. Spray waffle maker on top side. Put sprinkles of mozzarella at bottom of waffle maker to help make it crispy. Cook 1/3 of Chaffle mix. Remove Chaffle and follow the same instructions for the second and third Chaffles. Do NOT peek! Wait until all steam is gone.
4. I cooked each Chaffle for 3 minutes. This is a good time to make the topping.
5. Microwave the strawberries until soft. Mash with banana. Add ricotta and mash together.
6. Place the crispy side face down onto plate and put topping on the softer side.

Quinoa Flakes Breakfast Bread Chaffles

Makes 2 savory breakfast Chaffles in mini waffle maker. It tastes like bread! Provides complete grain and complete protein for breakfast.

Ingredients for Chaffles:

- 1 large egg, beaten (1/2 protein)
- 1 oz uncooked quinoa flakes
- 1 oz Ricotta (1/4 protein)
- 1/2 tsp onion powder
- 1/2 tsp garlic powder
- 1/8 tsp seasoned sea salt
- dash dried parsley

Ingredients to Reserve:

- 0.25 oz fresh parmesan, shredded (1/8 protein), for sprinkles
- oil spray

Ingredients for Topping:

- *"Nicole's Mock Sour Cream"*

  Use 1 oz Greek yogurt (1/8 protein) mixed with a dash each of seasoned sea salt, onion powder, and garlic powder.

  Sprinkle dried parsley on top of mock sour cream once served.

Instructions:

1. Heat mini waffle maker. Make sure you place a plate underneath to catch the mess.
2. Make Chaffle mix. You will use half of the mix for each Chaffle.
3. Spray waffle maker on top side. Put sprinkles of parmesan at bottom of waffle maker to help make it crispy. Cook 1/2 of Chaffle mix. Remove Chaffle and follow the same instructions for the second Chaffle. Do Not peek! Wait until all steam is gone.
4. Make topping while Chaffles are cooking.
5. Cool Chaffles 1-2 minutes on a wire cooling rack before adding topping.

Notes: Serve with 6 oz fruit for a complete breakfast. Instead of adding topping, you could add 0.25 oz more cheese for sprinkles. These should freeze well. I also made a sweet version and prefer the savory with quinoa flakes.

Peanut Butter Banana Chaffles

Makes 3 breakfast Chaffles in mini waffle maker. Provides complete protein, grain, and fruit. This will work in a large waffle maker.

Ingredients for Chaffles:

- 1 large egg, beaten (1/2 protein)
- 1 oz uncooked oats (full grain)
- 2 oz banana, mashed
- 0.5 oz peanut butter (1/4 protein) I used crunchy peanut butter.
- 1/2 tsp vanilla extract

Ingredients to Reserve:

- 0.5 oz mozzarella cheese, shredded (1/4 protein), for sprinkles.
- oil spray

Ingredients for Topping:

- 2 oz banana, mashed
- 2 oz frozen strawberries, cooked in the microwave until slightly syrupy

Instructions:

1. Heat mini waffle maker. Place a plate underneath to catch the mess.
2. Mix all Chaffle ingredients thoroughly to make sure peanut butter is mixed in well.
3. Spray top of waffle maker. Put 1/3 mozzarella sprinkles on bottom of waffle maker. Put THIRD of mixture into Dash.
4. Don't peek! Wait until all steam is gone. Cook longer to make it crispier. Repeat the same instructions for second and third Chaffles.
5. Let set for two minutes to get even crispier.
6. Place crispy side down on plate.

Topping: Mash the strawberries and banana together and spoon onto each Chaffle. I love peanut butter on banana, so initially I wasn't planning on putting the strawberries/banana on top, but I love that combo too! Problem solved. Do both! Or top with blueberries.

Cherry Almond Butter Chaffles

Makes 3 breakfast Chaffles cooked in mini waffle maker. Provides complete grain, protein, and fruit. This would work in a large waffle maker.

Ingredients for Chaffles:

- 1 large egg, beaten (1/2 protein)
- 1 oz uncooked oats (full grain)
- 2.5 oz frozen cherries, defrosted, and cut into small pieces. Remove all liquid and pat with a paper towel.
- 1 oz banana, mashed (used as a sweetener)
- 0.5 oz almond butter (1/4 protein) I used crunchy almond butter.
- 1/2 tsp almond extract
- 1/8 tsp cinnamon

Ingredients to Reserve:

- 0.5 oz mozzarella cheese, shredded (1/4 protein), for sprinkles
- oil spray

Ingredients for Topping:

- 2 oz frozen cherries, defrosted, including juice
- 0.5 oz banana, mashed (used as a sweetener)
- 1/2 tsp almond extract

Instructions:

Note: For the Chaffle mix, don't defrost the cherries so much that they cook. For the topping, you will want them slightly cooked so they will be softer and have lots of juice.

1. Heat mini waffle maker. Place plate underneath waffle maker to catch mess.
2. Mix all Chaffle ingredients thoroughly to make sure almond butter is mixed in well.
3. Spray top of waffle maker. Put 1/3 mozzarella sprinkles on bottom of waffle maker. Put THIRD of mixture into waffle maker. Don't peek! Wait until all steam is gone. Cook longer to make it crispier. Repeat same instructions for second and third Chaffles. Let set for two minutes to get even crispier. Place crispy side down on plate.

Topping: Mash banana and mix with defrosted cherries, mash slightly. Add almond extract.

This was delicious and had a fabulous texture too! When our kids were young, and we did road trips with no place to eat in sight, we'd finally stop to get something similar for breakfast and really enjoyed it. Years later I started making it from home, much to the delight of my family. Here is my no flour version.

Egg NicChaffles

Makes 2 breakfast Chaffles for a sandwich in waffle maker. Provides complete breakfast grain and complete protein. This recipe won't work in a large waffle maker.

Ingredients for Chaffles:

- **Important!** You need 2 MEDIUM eggs (3/4 protein). RESERVE one egg for inside sandwich. Beat the other egg for the mix. Eggs must weigh no more than 1.5 oz each.
- 1 oz uncooked oats (1 grain)
- 1/2 tsp garlic powder
- 1/2 tsp onion powder
- 1/8 tsp seasoned sea salt

Ingredients to Reserve:

- 0.5 oz cheddar cheese, shredded, (1/4 protein), for sprinkles.
- oil spray

Instructions:

1. Crack egg and weigh it. My medium eggs weigh 1.5 oz. If it's a tad more, just remove some of the egg white. A large egg won't work.
2. Heat mini waffle maker. Keep a plate underneath Dash to catch any mess.
3. Mix ONE egg, oats, and seasoning. Reserve the cheese!
4. Spray oil on top of waffle maker. Put HALF of the cheddar cheese sprinkles on bottom of waffle maker to make it crispy. Cook half the batter, remove, and follow the same instructions for the second half of Chaffle.
5. While second Chaffle is cooking, use a microwave POACHED egg maker to cook the sandwich egg, or cook how you'd like. You can even crack an egg into waffle maker and cook in there. (Be aware though because the egg can run completely off the mini waffle maker). I added some seasoned sea salt to my poached egg once cooked.

Notes:

1. Men can add a slice of cheese to sandwich for extra protein.
2. Serve with 6oz fruit.

Absolutely delicious and easy! Tastes like toast. Complete breakfast with addition of fruit.

Crispy Garlic Knot Chaffles

Makes 2 breakfast Chaffles in mini waffle maker. Provides complete grain and complete protein.

Ingredients for Chaffles:

- 1 large egg, beaten (1/2 protein)
- 1 oz uncooked oats (full grain)
- 0.5 oz mozzarella or cheddar cheese, shredded (1/4 protein)
- 1/4 tsp garlic granules (or garlic powder)
- 1 large garlic clove, minced
- dash sea salt

Ingredients to Reserve:

- 0.5 oz mozzarella or cheddar cheese, shredded (1/4 protein), for sprinkles
- oil spray (optional for this recipe since cheese will go on both sides)

Instructions:

1. Heat mini waffle maker. Make sure you place a plate underneath to catch mess.
2. Mix Chaffle ingredients and divide in half.
3. Put a FEW sprinkles of cheese on bottom of waffle maker, cover with HALF of mix and put a few more sprinkles of cheese on top of mix. Cook. Wait until all steam is gone. The longer you cook it, the crispier it gets, but putting sprinkles of cheese first and last will also make it crispier.
4. Repeat for second Chaffle.
5. Place on wire cooling rack for 1-2 minutes.

Notes:

1. You could make the same thing at lunch or dinner and leave out the oats, but I prefer this one.
2. Add 6 oz fruit for a complete and easy breakfast.

Not long ago, I was waking up at 5:30am to get to work and would just throw boring, dry cereal in a container and eat it with a banana on my way to work. So, I thought this simple and yummy breakfast might be a good alternative for some of you on the go and something the kids might like too!

Peanut Butter Toast Chaffles

Makes 2 breakfast Chaffles cooked in mini waffle maker. Provides complete protein and grain. These are great frozen, toasted in toaster or air fryer, and for a breakfast to go. Grab fruit to go with it, like a banana, and voilà! Tastes like toast.

Ingredients for Chaffles:

- 1 large egg, beaten (1/2 protein)
- 1 oz ricotta cheese (1/4 protein) (optional, helps to moisten)
- 1 oz banana, mashed (used as a sweetener & to moisten) (optional)
- 0.5 oz peanut butter (1/4 protein)
- 1 oz uncooked oats (full grain)
- 1/4 tsp cinnamon
- 1 tsp vanilla extract

Ingredient to Reserve:

- oil spray

Instructions:

1. Heat mini waffle maker. Place plate underneath to catch mess.
2. Mix Chaffle ingredients thoroughly to make sure peanut butter is mixed in well.
3. Spray top and bottom of waffle maker. Put HALF mixture into waffle maker. Cook until steam is gone. Don't peek! Cook longer to make it crispier.
4. Repeat same instructions for second Chaffle.
5. Cool for 1-2 minutes on wire cooling rack to get even crispier.

Note: Serve with 5 oz fruit or fruit compote on top of toast.

Who doesn't love rice at breakfast? This one uses Arborio rice (risotto rice). It was very tasty! You see the Chaffle at the back? Well, that's the crispier one because I remembered to put mozzarella on the mini waffle maker before adding the mix. It makes a huge difference! Also, cannot stress enough how helpful it is to put a plate underneath your mini waffle maker to help with any mess.

Italian Rice Chaffles

Makes 3 breakfast Chaffles in mini waffle maker. Provides complete protein and grain. Would work in a large waffle maker.

Ingredients for Chaffles:

- 4 oz precooked Arborio rice, risotto style rice (full grain)
- 1 large egg, beaten (1/2 protein)
- 0.5 oz fresh parmesan cheese, shredded (1/4 protein)
- 1/2 tsp Italian seasoning
- 1/4 tsp seasoned sea salt
- 1/4 tsp garlic powder

Ingredients to Reserve:

- 0.5 oz mozzarella cheese, shredded (1/4 protein), for sprinkles
- oil spray

Ingredient for topping:

- crushed red pepper once cooked (optional)

Instructions:

1. Heat mini waffle maker. Use a plate underneath to help with mess.
2. Mix Chaffle ingredients. Divide into thirds.
3. Spray waffle maker. Put a FEW sprinkles of mozzarella cheese onto bottom of waffle maker, cover with 1/3 mix and cook. Wait until all steam is gone. Do not peek! The longer you cook it, the crispier it gets, but putting sprinkles of cheese first will also make it crispier.
4. Cook for 3 minutes.
5. Repeat the same instructions for the second and third Chaffles.

Note: For a complete breakfast add 6 oz fruit.

Chunky breakfast Chaffle potato creation was delicious! My husband is Swiss-Italian, born and raised in Switzerland, and he really liked it too! Swiss would be more likely to eat whole potato or potato pieces than grated potato (like hash brown potatoes).

Swiss Potato Chaffles

Makes 2 thick breakfast Chaffles in mini waffle maker. Provides complete protein and complete grain. You might be able to use a large waffle iron instead.

Ingredients for Chaffles:

- 4 oz precooked potato, baked & peeled (full grain)
- 1 large egg, beaten (1/2 protein)
- 1 oz Swiss cheese grated (1/2 protein)- I used sliced Swiss cheese, cut into tiny pieces, since that is what I had.
- 1/2 tsp seasoned sea salt
- 1/4 tsp onion powder
- 1/4 tsp garlic granules (or powder)
- 1 tsp dried thyme
- 1/2 TBSP fresh thyme (or 1/4 tsp dried thyme)

Ingredient to Reserve:

- oil spray

Instructions:

1. Cook potato for 10 minutes in microwave with a paper towel around potato. Peel once cooked. Weigh out 4 oz, then dice into small chunks (do NOT mash potatoes) about the size of the tip of your thumb. Add seasoned sea salt, onion powder, and garlic granules to POTATOES before adding other ingredients. Mix and make sure seasoning is coated on potatoes or your potatoes won't have enough flavor.
2. Heat mini waffle maker. Make sure to put a plate under your waffle maker to minimize mess.
3. Cut sliced cheese into tiny pieces or use shredded Swiss cheese.
4. Mix Chaffle ingredients. Divide mix into half. Spray both sides of waffle maker. Put 1/2 mix into waffle maker and PRESS it down. Use a potholder, napkin, or towel, so you won't burn yourself. Wait until all steam is gone. The longer you cook it, the crispier it gets. Do not peek! Repeat the same instructions for the second Chaffle.
5. **I did not use cheese sprinkles for this recipe**. Place on wire cooling rack for 1-2 minutes.

Note: For a complete breakfast add 6 oz fruit

This was unique in flavor and very good!! I love things that are different from the usual, yet so very yummy too!

Rosemary Sweet Potato Chaffles

Makes 2 breakfast Chaffles in mini waffle maker. Provides complete breakfast protein and grain.

Ingredients for Chaffles:

- 4 oz precooked sweet potato, baked, peeled, & mashed (full grain)
- 1 large egg, beaten (1/2 protein)
- 0.5 oz fresh parmesan cheese, shredded (1/4 protein)
- 1/2 TBSP fresh rosemary (or 1/4 tsp dried rosemary)
- 1/4 tsp garlic granules (or powder)
- 1/4 tsp seasoned sea salt

Ingredients to Reserve:

- 0.5 oz mozzarella cheese, shredded (1/4 protein), for sprinkles
- oil spray

Instructions:

1. Heat mini waffle maker. Make sure to put a plate under your mini waffle maker to minimize mess.
2. Mix Chaffles ingredients and divide into half.
3. Spray waffle maker. Put a FEW sprinkles of mozzarella cheese onto bottom of waffle maker, cover with 1/2 mix and cook. Wait until all steam is gone. The longer you cook it, the crispier it gets, but putting sprinkles of cheese first will make it crispier too. Sweet potato is prone to sticking, so no peeking!
4. Repeat the same instructions for the second Chaffle.

Note: Serve with 6 oz fruit.

Peruvian Quinoa Chaffles

Makes 3 breakfast Chaffles in mini waffle maker or one large waffle in a large waffle maker. Provides complete protein and grain.

Ingredients for Chaffles:

- 4 oz precooked Quinoa (full grain)
- 1 large egg, beaten (1/2 protein)
- 0.5 oz mozzarella cheese, shredded (1/4 protein)
- 1 tsp onion powder
- 1/4 tsp sea salt
- 1/2 tsp cumin

Ingredients to Reserve:

- 0.5 oz mozzarella cheese, shredded (1/4 protein), for sprinkles
- oil spray

Instructions:

1. Heat mini waffle maker. Make sure to put a plate under waffle maker to minimize mess.
2. Spray top of waffle maker. Divide mix into thirds. Put a FEW sprinkles of mozzarella cheese onto waffle maker, cover with 1/3 mix and cook. Wait until all the steam is gone. The longer you cook it, the crispier it gets, but putting sprinkles of cheese first will make it crispier too.
3. Repeat the same instructions for the second and third Chaffles. Do not peek! Cook until steam is gone.
4. Place on a wire cooling rack for 1-2 minutes.

Note: For a complete breakfast add 6 oz fruit.

This one is so tasty and fun! Hubby and I were splitting my Chaffle creations and one Chaffle was eaten before this pic. This recipe actually makes 3 Chaffles.

Chinese Rice Chaffles

Makes 3 breakfast Chaffles in mini waffle maker or one waffle in a large waffle maker. Provides complete breakfast protein and grain.

Ingredients for Chaffles:

- 4 oz precooked rice (full grain)
- 1 large egg, beaten (1/2 protein)
- 0.5 oz mozzarella cheese, shredded (1/4 protein)
- 0.25 oz green onions, cut into tiny pieces, omit the white part (free condiment)
- 2 tsp BRAGG® Liquid Aminos (or GF soy sauce)
- 1/4 tsp ginger
- 1/4 garlic powder
- dash sea salt

Ingredients to Reserve:

- 0.5 oz mozzarella cheese, shredded (1/4 protein), for sprinkles
- oil spray

Ingredient for Topping:

- 1 TBSP green onions, chopped (free condiment)

Instructions:

1. Heat mini waffle maker. Make sure to put a plate under waffle maker to minimize mess.
2. Mix all Chaffle ingredients.
3. Spray top of waffle maker. Divide mix into thirds. Put a FEW sprinkles of mozzarella cheese onto bottom of waffle maker, cover with 1/3 mix and cook. Wait until all the steam is gone. The longer you cook it, the crispier it gets, but putting sprinkles of cheese first will make it crispier too. Do not peek!
4. Repeat the same instructions for the second and third Chaffles.
5. Place on a wire cooling rack for 1-2 minutes.

Note: For a complete breakfast add 6 oz fruit.

My new breakfast creation turned out absolutely amazing! So crispy that I was able to pick them up and eat with my hand and bursting with flavor at every bite! Wow!

Sweet Potato Blueberry Chaffles

Makes 3 breakfast Chaffles in mini waffle maker. Provides complete grain, complete protein, and complete fruit. This recipe would work in a large waffle maker.

Ingredients for Chaffles:

- 2 oz precooked sweet potato, baked, peeled, & mashed (1/2 grain)
- 1 large egg, beaten (1/2 protein)
- 1 oz banana, mashed (used as a sweetener)
- 1 oz blueberries, I used fresh organic blueberries.
- 0.5 oz uncooked oats (1/2 grain)
- 0.5 oz mozzarella cheese, shredded (1/4 protein)
- 1/4 tsp vanilla extract
- 1/4 tsp maple extract
- 1/8 tsp baking powder
- dash salt

Ingredients to Reserve:

- 0.5 oz mozzarella cheese, shredded (1/4 protein), for sprinkles
- oil spray

Ingredients for Topping:

- 2 oz blueberries, heated in microwave
- 2 oz banana

Note: Mash half of banana to put in blueberry topping and slice the other half for the top of blueberry topping.

Instructions:

1. Heat mini waffle maker. Make sure you place a plate underneath to catch mess.
2. Mash sweet potato and banana. Add other ingredients. Mix well. Divide mix into thirds.
3. Spray waffle maker on both sides. Sweet potato is prone to sticking. Put sprinkles of mozzarella at bottom of waffle maker to help make it crispy. Cook 1/3 of Chaffle mix. Remove Chaffle and follow the same instructions for the second and third Chaffles. Do NOT peek! Wait until all steam is gone. I cooked each Chaffle for 4 minutes.
4. Place the crispy side face down onto plate and put topping on the softer side.

Note: These would freeze and toast well.

These were very yummy and refreshing! Plus, they were crispy enough to eat with my hands. Fun fact: Due to climate, the only state in the US that can grow cashews is Hawaii. Note: Only 2 Chaffles shown, since one was eaten pre-pic! Extra pineapple and cashews in pic are for presentation only.

Taste of Hawaii Breakfast Chaffles

Makes breakfast 3 Chaffles in mini waffle maker. Provides complete grain, complete protein, and complete fruit. This recipe would work in a large waffle maker

Ingredients for Chaffles:

- 1 large egg, beaten (1/2 protein)
- 0.25 oz mozzarella, shredded (1/8 protein)
- 1 oz banana, mashed (used as a sweetener)
- 0.25 oz cashews, finely chopped, or cashew butter (1/8 protein)
- 1 oz uncooked oats (full grain)
- 1 tsp vanilla extract
- 1 tsp banana extract
- 1 tsp coconut extract
- dash of salt

Ingredients to Reserve:

- 0.5 oz mozzarella cheese, shredded (1/4 protein), for sprinkles
- 3 oz small pineapple rings, or approximately 3 small rings measured
- oil spray

Ingredient for Topping:

- 2 oz banana, sliced

Instructions:

1. Heat mini waffle maker. Make sure you place a plate underneath to catch mess.
2. Mix Chaffle ingredients. Divide mix into thirds.
3. Spray waffle maker on both sides. Pineapple is not forgiving; it is prone to sticking. Put sprinkles of mozzarella at bottom of waffle maker to help make it crispy. Cook 1/3 of Chaffle mix. Put a pineapple ring in the bottom of waffle maker and put mix in and around it. I used DOLE® pineapple slices from a 20 oz can. I prefer fresh, but they need to be small and thin. Remove Chaffle and follow the same instructions for the second and third Chaffles. Do NOT peek! Wait until all steam is gone.
4. I cooked each Chaffle for 3 1/2 minutes.
5. Place the crispy side face down onto plate and put sliced topping on the softer side.

Note: These would freeze and toast well.

Everywhere you go in Spain you will see Spanish Tortillas (Spanish Potato Omelette) and I've made them at home for years. Today, I decided to create a Chaffle version, and it came out delicious! It's not at all like hash browns, nor should it be.

Spanish Tortilla Chaffles

Makes 2 thick breakfast Chaffles in mini waffle maker. Thick ones will most resemble Spanish Omelettes. Provides complete grain and complete protein. This recipe can be made in a large waffle maker.

Ingredients for Chaffles:

- 4 oz precooked potato, baked, peeled, & cut into small pieces-not sliced like typical Spanish tortilla. It cooks better in a waffle maker this way.
- 1 large egg, beaten (1/2 protein)
- 0.5 oz mozzarella cheese, shredded (1/4 protein)
- 1 tsp butter extract
- 1 1/2 TBSP fresh thyme, or 1 tsp dried thyme

Note: Normally a Spanish Tortilla wouldn't have thyme, but I liked it.

- 1/4 salt
- 1/8 pepper

Ingredients to Reserve:

- 0.5 oz mozzarella cheese, shredded (1/4 protein), for sprinkles
- oil spray

Instructions:

1. Cut baked potato into small pieces. Weigh 4 oz.
2. Heat mini waffle maker. Make sure you place a plate underneath to catch mess.
3. Mix all Chaffle ingredients. Divide mix into half.
4. Spray mini waffle maker on both sides. Put sprinkles of mozzarella at bottom of waffle maker to help make it crispy. Cook 1/2 of Chaffle mix. Remove Chaffle and follow the same instructions for the second Chaffle. Do NOT peek! Wait until all steam is gone.
5. I cooked each Chaffle for 4 minutes.

Notes:

1. It's a debate whether to put sauteed onion in a Spanish Tortilla, so add it if you'd like, but it's not always added in Spain.
2. Serve with 6oz fruit for a complete breakfast.

When I taught high school French, I became obsessed with Crêpes! My students learned how to make Crêpes too. Mind you, I was not as obsessed as I am with Chaffles. Anyway, yesterday a lemon rolled out of the bag and when I picked it up, I had this new creation idea. Go figure.

Lemon Crêpe Chaffles

Makes 2 breakfast Chaffles in mini waffle maker. Provides complete breakfast grain and protein. Won't work in a large waffle maker. If you do this one in a large waffle maker, it WILL stick. This is meant to be tart and not so sweet.

Ingredients for Chaffles:

- 1 large egg, beaten (1/2 protein)
- 1 oz uncooked oats (full grain)
- 2 oz banana, mashed (used as a sweetener)
- 1 oz ricotta cheese (1/4 protein)
- 1 TBSP fresh squeezed lemon juice, for mix
- 1 tsp lemon zest (approx. 1 lemon)
- 1 tsp lemon extract
- 1 tsp vanilla extract
- dash of sea salt

Ingredients to Reserve:

- 0.5 oz fresh parmesan cheese, shredded (1/4 protein), for sprinkles
- oil spray

Ingredients for Topping:

- 4 oz fresh strawberries, cut into tiny pieces
- 1 TBSP fresh lemon juice on strawberries and mixed well before putting onto Chaffles

Note: If you prefer the topping less tarte, and sweeter, then use a mix of banana with the strawberry.

Instructions:

1. Heat mini waffle maker. Make sure you place a plate underneath to catch mess.
2. Mash banana. Mix all Chaffle ingredients. Divide in half.
3. Spray mini waffle maker on both sides. This Chaffle is not forgiving and could stick. Put sprinkles of mozzarella at bottom of waffle maker to help make it crispy and help it not to stick. Spread sprinkles around evenly. Cook 1/2 of Chaffle mix. Remove Chaffle and follow the same instructions for the second Chaffle. Do NOT peek! Wait until all steam is gone. Careful. This one will stick if you peek.
4. I cooked each Chaffle for 3 minutes.
5. Place the crispy side face down onto plate and put strawberry topping on the softer side.

Note: This is more like a light breakfast and is therefore good when you have a late breakfast and don't want to eat lunch too late.

This morning I took my Cherry Bliss Waffle creation and changed it into Chaffles. It's a family favorite!

Cherry Bliss Chaffles

Makes 3 breakfast Chaffles in mini waffle maker. Provides complete grain, complete protein, and complete fruit. This recipe will work in a large waffle maker. This recipe requires more steps for the topping, but it's worth every minute!

Ingredients for Chaffles:

- 1 large egg, beaten (1/2 protein)
- 1 oz uncooked oats (full grain)
- 2.5 oz banana, mashed
- 2 oz frozen cherries, defrosted, and cut in half
- 1/3 tsp almond extract
- 1/3 tsp vanilla extract
- 1/4 tsp baking powder
- 1/8 tsp baking soda
- dash sea salt
- 1/8 tsp Chai spice, (or cinnamon)
- 1/4 tsp dried instant coffee

Ingredients to Reserve:

- 0.5 oz mozzarella cheese, shredded (1/4 protein), for sprinkles
- oil spray

Ingredients for Topping:

- 0.5 oz banana, mashed
- 0.25 oz almond butter (1/8 protein)
- 1 oz Greek yogurt (1/8 protein)
- 1 oz frozen cherries, left whole and defrosted
- 1/8 tsp almond extract

Chaffle Instructions:

1. Heat mini waffle maker. Place a plate underneath to catch any mess.
2. Mash banana and mix with other ingredients. Add cherries after adding the spices. You can either add a pinch of each of the spices to make it easier, or you can use my precise measurements.
3. Spray top of waffle maker. Sprinkle some of the mozzarella on the bottom of waffle maker for each of the 3 Chaffles to help make them crispy.
4. When you pour in batter, move cherries around evenly before closing, so you won't get all the cherries in the middle.
5. This makes 3 Chaffles. Make sure and don't open until all steam is gone. No peeking.
6. Prepare topping while Chaffles are cooking.

Topping Instructions:

1. Step 1: Mash 0.5 oz banana with 0.25 oz almond butter, and 1 oz Greek yogurt. Put this creamy mixture on top of Chaffles, in the middle, and spread when ready to eat.
2. Step 2: Defrost 1 oz frozen cherries (keep whole) defrosted in a microwave and add 1/8 tsp (or dash) of almond extract. Put this on top of creamy mixture, including any juice made from defrosting cherries.

Note: Side with 4 oz fruit of your choice and 6 oz veggies.

Dutch Apple Chaffles

Makes 3 breakfast Chaffles in mini waffle maker. Provides complete breakfast grain, complete protein, and complete fruit. This recipe should not be made in a large waffle maker, because it will fall apart. You need a small, 4-inch waffle maker.

Ingredients for Chaffles:

- 1 large egg, beaten (1/2 protein)
- 0.5 oz Gouda cheese, shredded (1/4 protein)
- 1 oz uncooked oats (1 grain)
- 2.5 oz apple shredded, that has all the water squeezed out of it. Important! Measure after squeezing.
- 1 oz banana, mashed (used as a sweetener)
- 0.5 oz plain applesauce
- 1 tsp vanilla extract
- 1/2 tsp butter extract
- 1/2 tsp cinnamon
- 1/8 tsp cardamom
- dash salt

Ingredients to Reserve:

- 0.5 oz Gouda, shredded (1/4 protein), for sprinkles
- oil spray

Ingredients for Topping:

- 2 oz apple, diced into tiny pieces

Instructions:

1. Peel and shred about 6 oz of apple. Squeeze out all water. Weigh 2.5 oz after squeezing.
2. Heat mini waffle maker. Make sure you place a plate underneath to catch mess.
3. Mash banana and add other ingredients. Mix well and divide into thirds.
4. Spray mini waffle maker on BOTH sides for this recipe. Put sprinkles of Gouda at bottom of waffle maker to help make it crispy. Cook 1/3 of Chaffle mix. Remove Chaffle and follow the same instructions for the second and third Chaffles. Do NOT peek! Wait until all steam is gone.
5. I cooked each Chaffle for 4 minutes. This is a good time to make the topping.
6. Place the crispy side face down onto plate and put topping on the softer side.

Note: You can fold like a taco to eat.

LUNCH

So tasty! These are full of flavor and are light and refreshing. Best for a light lunch with added veggies, or soup and fruit.

Caprese Bruschetta Chaffles

Makes 2 lunch Chaffles in mini waffle maker. Provides complete protein, complete fat, and 1.5 oz veggies. Won't work in a large waffle maker. Very light, flavorful, and refreshing!

Ingredients for Chaffles:

- 1 large egg, beaten (1/2 protein)
- 0.5 oz fresh parmesan cheese, shredded (1/2 fat)
- 1/2 tsp garlic powder
- 1/8 tsp seasoned sea salt

Ingredients to Reserve:

- 0.5 oz fresh parmesan cheese, shredded (1/2 fat), for sprinkles
- oil spray

Ingredients for Topping:

- 1 oz cherry size FRESH mozzarella cheese balls, cut into small pieces (1/2 protein)
- 1 garlic clove, minced, 1/2 for each Chaffle
- 1.5 oz cherry tomatoes cut into 4 pieces each and with a dash of salt
- fresh basil
- a spray of olive oil (optional)

Instructions:

1. Cut tomatoes and place on paper towel to catch excess water. Mince garlic. Cut fresh mozzarella cheese balls. Chiffonnade the basil.
2. Heat mini waffle maker. Make sure you place a plate underneath to catch mess.
3. Mix all Chaffle ingredients. Divide mix in half.
4. Spray top of mini waffle maker. Put sprinkles of parmesan at bottom of waffle maker to help make it crispy. Cook half Chaffle mix. Remove Chaffle, spray top of waffle maker, and cook other half of mix. Remove Chaffle.
5. Put minced garlic directly onto each Chaffle. Put in air fryer for 8 minutes (approximately) at 390 degrees or use a toaster oven.
6. Once toasted remove. Put cut up cheese on top, followed by tomatoes, and spray with olive oil spray if you'd like. Add fresh basil.

Note: At lunch add 4.4 oz veggies and 6 oz fruit. I recommend these at lunch because they are light.

Egg Whites Spinach Chaffles

Makes 2 thin, lunch Chaffles, in mini waffle maker. Provides complete protein and 0.3 oz veggies. Will not work in a large waffle maker. Egg whites don't puff up like whole eggs, so these are thin.

Ingredients for Chaffles:

- 2 oz egg whites, beaten (1/2 protein) I used the whites of 3 small eggs.
- 0.3 oz fresh, whole, raw, baby spinach, with stems removed (about 8 leaves per Chaffle)
- 0.5 oz mozzarella cheese, shredded (1/4 protein)
- 1/2 tsp garlic powder
- 1/2 tsp onion powder
- 1/8 tsp seasoned sea salt

Ingredients to Reserve:

- 0.5 oz mozzarella cheese, shredded (1/4 protein), for sprinkles
- oil spray

Instructions:

1. Heat mini waffle maker. Make sure you place a plate underneath to catch mess.
2. Mix Chaffle ingredients. You will need a spoon to put mix in waffle maker, since this is more liquid than with egg yolk and doesn't divide in half well.
3. Spray top of waffle maker so spinach won't stick. Put cheese sprinkles at bottom of waffle maker to make it crispy.
4. Place half of spinach leaves, raw on top of mix. Close waffle maker. Cook half Chaffle mix. Remove Chaffle and follow the same instructions for the second Chaffle.

Notes:

1. This will be thinner than a whole egg with yolk Chaffle. Don't be concerned if the egg mix doesn't cover up Dash completely. It still makes two.
2. Add 5.7 oz veggies, 1 fat, and 6 oz fruit for a complete lunch, or you could count both cheeses as a fat and add 2 oz protein to your lunch or add more cheese to Chaffle.

Hominy Chaffles

Makes 3 lunch Chaffles in a mini waffle maker. Provides complete protein and 6 oz veggies. Has a wonderful texture and is very filling! Would work in a large waffle maker.

Ingredients for Chaffles:

- 1 large egg, beaten (1/2 protein)
- 5 oz Mexican style canned hominy, well drained
- 1 oz pickled jalapeños, sliced (free condiment)
- 0.50 oz cheddar cheese, shredded (1/4 protein)
- 1 tsp onion powder
- 1 tsp garlic powder
- 1/8 tsp seasoned sea salt

Ingredients to Reserve:

- 0.5 oz cheddar cheese, shredded (1/4 protein), for sprinkles
- oil spray

Instructions:

1. Heat mini waffle maker. Make sure you place a plate underneath to catch mess.
2. Mix all Chaffle ingredients.
3. Spray waffle maker on top side. Put sprinkles of cheddar cheese at bottom of waffle maker to help make it crispy. Cook 1/3 of Chaffle mix. Remove Chaffle and follow the same instructions for the second and third Chaffles. Do NOT peek! Wait until all steam is gone.
4. Cook each Chaffle for 4 minutes, or longer, if you want it crispier.

Note: Serve with 6 oz fruit.

At restaurants in France, it's common to have a salad at lunch with warm goat cheese on toast. When creating this Chaffle, I was hoping to make something similar. It turned out to be delicious!

Goat Cheese French Chaffles

Makes 2 lunch Chaffles in mini waffle maker. Provides complete protein and complete fat. Won't work in a large waffle maker.

Ingredients for Chaffles:

- 1 large egg, beaten (1/2 protein)
- 1 oz goat cheese (1/2 protein)
- 1/4 tsp Herbes de Provence
- 1/4 tsp Fleur de Sel (or sea salt)
- 1/2 tsp green onion, cut in tiny pieces, or 1/2 tsp dried chives, (free condiment)

Ingredient to Reserve:

- 1 oz mozzarella cheese, shredded (full fat), for sprinkles

Note: You will put sprinkles of cheese on the bottom of waffle maker AND on top of mix once in waffle maker. This will make it crusty like toast. Make sure and reserve enough mozzarella sprinkles for second Chaffle.

Instructions:

1. Heat mini waffle maker. Make sure you place a plate underneath to catch mess.
2. Mix all Chaffle ingredients. Divide mix in half.
3. You don't need to spray waffle maker since you will be putting sprinkles of cheese. Put sprinkles of mozzarella at bottom of waffle maker to help make it crispy and on top of mix. This will also make it like toast. Cook half Chaffle mix. Remove Chaffle and follow the same instructions for the second Chaffle.
4. Cool for 1-2 minutes on a wire cooling rack.

Note: Add 6 oz veggies and 6 oz fruit for a complete lunch. Pairs well with a salad that has fat free vinaigrette.

I absolutely love Spanakopita, so I decided to create something close to it and it turned out so yummy!! Spanakopita is Greek Spinach Pie and it's chock FULL of spinach! If you love, love, love spinach, then you will love this!

Spanakopita Chaffles

Makes 2 lunch Chaffles in mini waffle maker. Provides complete protein, complete fat, and 2.7 oz veggies. I would not suggest for a large waffle maker, it would stick!

Ingredients for Chaffles:

- 1.5 oz cooked Spinach with all the water squeezed out, like cauliflower rice for pizza crust! I started with a whole bag of 6 oz fresh spinach that becomes 1.5 oz once cooked
- 1 large egg, beaten (1/2 protein)
- 1 oz Feta cheese crumbles (1/2 protein)
- 1 oz onion, finely chopped
- 1 oz fresh green onion, chopped
- 1 clove garlic, minced (0.1 oz)
- 1/8 tsp dried dill (optional)
- 1/8 tsp dried parsley
- 1/8 tsp onion powder
- 1/8 tsp garlic powder
- 1/4 tsp salt (I sprinkled more salt upon serving).
- 1/4 tsp butter extract

Ingredients to Reserve:

- 1 oz mozzarella cheese shredded (full fat), for sprinkles on bottom of waffle maker and on top of mix once in waffle maker. This will save it from sticking and make it crispy. Make sure and reserve enough mozzarella sprinkles for the second Chaffle.
- oil spray

Instructions:

1. Spray a pan with oil and cook spinach until wilted. Once wilted, remove from heat, and squeeze it to death until no excess water left. Chop up the spinach.
2. Spray clean pan and cook onion, garlic, and green onion.
3. Heat mini waffle maker. Make sure you place a plate underneath to catch mess.
4. Put all the Feta in a bowl with the egg, mix well until there are no large chunks. Don't use a hand mixer! Add spinach, onion/garlic mixture to egg and Feta. Add seasonings. Mix well. Divide in half.
5. Spray top AND bottom of waffle maker. Put sprinkles of mozzarella at bottom of waffle maker and on top of mix to help make it crispy. Cook half Chaffle mix. Remove Chaffle and follow the same instructions for the second Chaffle. Do NOT peek! Wait until all steam is gone. About 4 minutes each.

   Note: Complete lunch with addition of 3.3 oz veggies and 6 oz fruit.

I had been wanting to make my carrot/cauliflower rice waffle recipe into Chaffles. This was so tasty and such a nice change of pace for a lunch! I ate it as a double decker sandwich, or you could eat it as three open faced sandwiches. Carrots and cauliflower in pic are only for presentation.

Carrot/Cauliflower Rice Chaffles Tuna Sandwich

Makes 3 lunch Chaffles in the mini waffle maker for open faced sandwiches, or one double decker sandwich. This also works well in a large waffle maker, but you need the kind with high heat setting. Provides complete veggies, complete protein, and complete fat.

Ingredients for Chaffles:

- 3 oz cooked carrots, mashed (1/2 veggie)
- 3 oz frozen cauliflower rice, defrosted and strained of water: Start with 7 oz frozen cauliflower rice and squeeze to death to get all water out, (1/2 veggie). I prefer WHOLE FOODS® cauliflower rice.
- 1 large egg, beaten (1/2 protein)
- 0.5 oz fresh parmesan cheese shredded (1/2 fat). This helps to bind the cauliflower. No cheese sprinkles.
- 1 tsp "Everything but the Bagel" seasoning
- 1/4 tsp cumin

Ingredient to Reserve:

- oil spray

Ingredients for Sandwich Filling:

- 2 oz canned tuna (1/2 protein)
- 1/2 TBSP mayonnaise (1/2 fat), added to tuna
- dash season sea salt added to tuna

Ingredient for Topping:

- red pepper flakes (optional)

Instructions:

1. Heat mini waffle maker. Make sure and have a plate under it to catch the mess.
2. Mix Chaffle ingredients and divide into thirds.
3. Spray waffle maker on BOTH SIDES. Carrots and cauliflower rice stick! No peeking!
4. Cook 1/3 of Chaffle mix. Remove Chaffle. Repeat the same instructions for second and third Chaffles.
5. Prepare sandwich filling while Chaffles are cooking.

Notes:

1. These Chaffles need to be crisped up in the air fryer before you add the tuna. Or, you could add less tuna and sprinkle some mozzarella onto the waffle maker, so it will be crispier.
2. For a complete lunch add 6 oz fruit.

This recipe blew me away! The pears tasted caramelized and there's just a tad of sweetness, sweet and savory all in one. This would combine nicely with a salad.

Pear, Blackberry, & Brie Chaffles

Makes 3 lunch Chaffles in mini waffle maker. Would work in a large waffle maker. Provides complete fat, complete protein, and 4 oz fruit.

Ingredients for Chaffles:

- 1 large egg, beaten (1/2 protein)
- 2 oz fresh pear, not very ripe, peeled & sliced thinly
- 2 oz fresh blackberries (about 3 berries for each Chaffle)
- 1 oz fresh Brie cheese, cut into tiny pieces (full fat)
- 1 tsp vanilla extract
- 1/2 tsp cinnamon
- dash nutmeg
- dash sea salt

Ingredients to Reserve:

- 1 oz mozzarella cheese, shredded (1/2 protein), for sprinkles
- oil spray

Instructions:

1. Cut Brie into tiny pieces right away. Separate the pieces or they will melt together. Leaving it out of fridge for only a few minutes will make it soft and more difficult to cut into tiny pieces.
2. Heat mini waffle maker. Make sure you place a plate underneath to catch mess.
3. Peel pear, core, and slice thinly.
4. Mix all Chaffle ingredients. Make sure and cover pear and berries in egg and Brie.
5. It's not easy to divide this mix. Just make sure that each Chaffle has the same amount of mix, and about 3 berries per Chaffle. Since the pears become caramelized your waffle maker will be a mess, but it's absolutely worth it!
6. Spray waffle maker on the top side. Put sprinkles of mozzarella at bottom of waffle maker to help make it crispy. Cook 1/3 of Chaffle mix. Remove Chaffle and follow the same instructions for the second and third Chaffles. Do NOT peek! Wait until all steam is gone.
7. Cook each Chaffle for 4 minutes, or longer, if you want it crispier. Place on a wire cooling rack to cool for 1-2 minutes to help make it crispy.

Note: Serve with 2 oz fruit.

Pumpkin Cheesecake Chaffles

Makes 3 lunch Chaffles in mini waffle maker. Provides complete protein, fruit, and fat for lunch. Will work in a large waffle maker.

Ingredients for Chaffles:

- 1 large egg, beaten (1/2 protein)
- 1 oz cream cheese (1 full fat). Whipped cream cheese is easier.
- 2.5 oz canned pumpkin purée
- 1.5 oz banana, mashed (used as a sweetener)
- 1/2 tsp pumpkin pie spice
- 1/2 tsp cinnamon
- 1 tsp vanilla extract
- 1/3 tsp baking powder

Ingredient to Reserve:

- oil spray

Ingredients for Topping:

- 0.5 oz peanut butter (1/4 protein)
- 1 oz ricotta cheese (1/4 protein)
- 1 oz banana, mashed
- 1 oz canned pumpkin
- dash pumpkin pie spice
- dash nutmeg

Instructions:

1. Heat mini waffle maker. Place a plate underneath to catch mess.
2. Mash and mix all Chaffle ingredients well.
3. Spray waffle maker with oil on both sides. Pumpkin tends to stick! Add 1/3 of the mix. Cook until steam is gone. No peeking! Pumpkin does not forgive peeking! Repeat instructions for second and third Chaffles. Cook each Chaffle for 4 minutes.
4. Prepare topping as the Chaffles cook. Mash all topping ingredients together.
5. Place on a wire cooling rack for 1-2 minutes. This is *not* a crispy Chaffle, it's soft.
6. Layer the Chaffles with topping on each layer or place topping on each Chaffle like the photo.

Note: For a complete lunch add 6 oz vegetables.

When your family smells these, they will want some too!

Pecan Butter Bananas Foster Chaffles

Makes 3 lunch Chaffles in the mini waffle maker. Provides complete protein, fruit, and fat. A large waffle maker would work for this.

Ingredients for Chaffles:

- 1 large egg, beaten (1/2 protein)
- 1.5 oz precooked quinoa (3/8 protein)
- 0.25 oz mozzarella cheese, shredded (1/8 protein)
- 2 oz banana, mashed
- 0.25 oz pecan butter (1/2 fat) See recipe in back of cookbook.
- 1 tsp vanilla extract
- 1/2 tsp cinnamon
- 1/8 tsp butter extract

Ingredient to Reserve:

- oil spray

Ingredients for Topping:

- 4 oz banana, mashed
- 0.25 pecan butter (1/2 fat)
- 1/4 tsp vanilla extract
- 1/8 tsp rum extract (optional)
- dash nutmeg
- dash cinnamon

Instructions:

1. Heat mini waffle maker. Make sure you place a plate underneath to catch mess.
2. Mix Chaffle ingredients and divide into thirds.
3. Spray waffle maker on both sides. **No cheese sprinkles for this recipe.** Cook 1/3 of Chaffle mix. Remove Chaffle and follow the same instructions for the second and third Chaffles. Do NOT peek! Wait until all steam is gone.
4. Make topping while Chaffles are cooking.
5. Place Chaffles on a wire cooling rack to cool 1-2 minutes
6. Mash topping ingredients together well. Warm in microwave. Spread topping on Chaffles.

Note: You can substitute pecan butter with another nut butter, but it won't have the authentic southern taste. Pecan butter is easy to make! Serve with 6 oz veggies.

Churros

Makes 3 lunch Chaffles in mini waffle maker. Can be made in a large waffle maker. Provides complete protein, complete fat, and half fruit.

Ingredients for Chaffles:

- 1 large egg, beaten (1/2 protein)
- 3 oz banana, very mashed
- 1 tsp vanilla extract
- 1/2 tsp cinnamon
- 1/8 tsp baking powder
- dash of baking soda

Ingredients to Reserve:

- 1 oz mozzarella cheese, shredded, for sprinkles only! (1/2 protein)
- oil spray

Ingredient for Topping:

- generous amount of cinnamon

Instructions:

1. Heat mini waffle maker. Make sure you place a plate underneath to catch mess.
2. Mix Chaffle ingredients and divide into thirds.
3. Spray waffle maker on top side. Put sprinkles of mozzarella at bottom of waffle maker to help make it crispy. Cook 1/3 of Chaffle mix. Remove Chaffle and follow the same instructions for the second and third Chaffles. Do NOT peek! Wait until all steam is gone.
4. Slice into strips. Put crunchy side up and press down with a sharp, serrated knife to cut. This helps not to tear it and have even strips.
5. Sprinkle generously on both sides with cinnamon.
6. Place 1-2 minutes on a wire cooling rack.

Note: Serve with 6 oz veggies.

We have been making tiramisù in our house for years. My sister-in-law, Annie, taught me how to make it. Years later, my husband got a different recipe from a good friend and became famous for his tiramisù. I knew that I would have to figure out a no sugar, no flour Chaffle version and hubby loves this one!

Tiramisù Chaffles

Makes 3 "thin" lunch Chaffles in mini waffle maker. Provides full protein, full fat, and 3 oz fruit. These are not crispy, nor should they be.

Ingredients for Chaffles:

- 1 large egg, beaten (1/2 protein)
- 2 oz banana mashed (used as a sweetener). Don't add more.
- 0.5 oz mascarpone cheese (1/2 fat)
- 0.5 oz mozzarella cheese, shredded (1/4 protein)
- 1 tsp instant coffee powder (I made my instant coffee granules into a powder using my mini food processor).
- 1 tsp vanilla extract
- 1 tsp rum extract

Ingredient to Reserve:

- oil spray

Ingredients for Topping:

- 1 oz banana mashed (used as a sweetener) Don't add more.
- 0.5 oz mascarpone cheese (1/2 fat)
- 1 oz ricotta cheese (1/4 protein)
- dash vanilla extract
- 1/2 tsp instant coffee powder

Instructions:

1. Heat mini waffle maker. Make sure you place a plate underneath to catch mess.
2. Mash banana and mascarpone together, then add other Chaffle ingredients. Don't be tempted to add more banana or you will compromise the tiramisù taste. Mix very well and divide into thirds.

Note: No cheese sprinkles in this recipe. It's better this way.

3. Spray waffle maker on BOTH sides. Cook 1/3 of Chaffle mix. Remove Chaffle and follow the same instructions for the second and third Chaffles. Do not peek! Wait until all steam is gone.
4. Place Chaffles on a wire cooling rack and don't put topping on until cooled for 3-5 minutes. Make topping while Chaffles are cooling.

Topping: Mash banana, mascarpone, and ricotta. Add other ingredients and mix well. Spread topping on Chaffles to completely cover the tops. I layered my Chaffles with topping on each layer.

Notes:

1. It's NOT recommended to eat these Chaffles refrigerated! Even though tiramisù is normally refrigerated and served cold. I tried them refrigerated and the taste was totally off, so I had to remake them.
2. Serve with 6 oz veggie and 3 oz fruit.

My husband bought "Jelly Berries" purple grapes and they were too sweet for me. I even researched them to make sure there wasn't any added sugar pumped inside. Nope. Apparently, they are a special variety that is in fact naturally sweeter than others. Then I had a thought that they might work as a mock grape jelly in a Chaffle, so my new creation was born! So yummy!

Peanut Butter & Grape Jelly Chaffles

Makes 2 lunch Chaffles with mini waffle maker. Provides complete protein, complete fat, and 2 oz fruit.

Ingredients for Chaffles:

- 1 TBSP crunchy peanut butter (full fat)
- 2 oz PURPLE grapes cut in half. I used Jelly Berries brand. They are too sweet for me to eat plain, but great for this!
- 1 large egg, beaten (1/2 protein)
- 0.5 oz mozzarella cheese, shredded (1/4 protein)
- dash salt (omit if you have salt in your peanut butter)

Ingredients to Reserve:

- 0.5 oz mozzarella cheese, shredded (1/4 protein), for sprinkles
- oil spray

Instructions:

1. Heat mini waffle maker. Make sure you place a plate underneath to catch mess.
2. Cut grapes in half. Mix all Chaffle ingredients. Divide in half.
3. Spray top of waffle maker. Put sprinkles of mozzarella at bottom of waffle maker to help make it crispy and help it not to stick. Spread sprinkles around evenly. Cook 1/2 of Chaffle mix. Remove Chaffle and follow the same instructions for the second Chaffle. Do NOT peek! Wait until all steam is gone.
4. I cooked each Chaffle for 3 minutes.

Note: Serve with 6 oz veggies and 4 oz fruit.

LUNCH/ DINNER

Lemon Dill Salmon Chaffles

Makes 2 lunch or dinner Chaffles in mini waffle maker or in a large waffle maker. Provides full protein and full fat.

Ingredients for Chaffles:

- 2 oz canned wild caught Alaskan pink salmon, or fresh, cooked salmon (1/2 protein)
- 1 large egg, beaten (1/2 protein)
- 1 TBSP fresh lemon juice
- 1/2 tsp dried dill weed
- 1/2 tsp garlic powder
- 1/2 tsp onion powder
- 1/8 tsp seasoned sea salt
- zest of one lemon

Ingredients to Reserve:

- 0.5 oz white cheddar slice for bottom of waffle maker only, like sprinkles are used. Cut slice in half and use half of slice for bottom of each Chaffle (1/2 fat)
- oil spray

Ingredients for Topping:

- 1/2 TBSP Tartar sauce (1/2 fat)
- lemon slice or wedge (optional)

Instructions:

1. Heat mini waffle maker. Make sure you place a plate underneath to catch mess.
2. Mix all Chaffle ingredients and divide in half.
3. Spray waffle maker on top and put 1/2 cheddar slice at bottom of waffle maker to help make it crispy. Cook 1/2 of Chaffle mix. Remove Chaffle and follow the same instructions for the second Chaffle. Do NOT peek! Wait until all steam is gone.
4. I cooked each Chaffle for 3 minutes.
5. Place the crispy side face down onto plate. Serve with Tartar sauce and lemon.

Note: Serve with 6 oz veggie and 6 oz fruit at lunch or 14 oz veggie at dinner.

Zucchini Fritters Chaffles

Makes 2 lunch or dinner Chaffles in mini waffle maker and provides complete protein, fat, and 2.5 oz veggies. Would not recommend in a large waffle maker.

Ingredients for Chaffles:

- 1 large egg, beaten (1/2 protein)
- 2.5 oz fresh grated zucchini that has been completely squeezed of all water. I started with 7 oz! You don't want moisture in it, or you will have mushy Chaffles that will stick.
- 0.5 oz fresh parmesan, shredded for mix (1/4 protein)
- 1/2 tsp onion powder
- 1/2 tsp garlic powder or granules
- 1/8 tsp seasoned sea salt

Ingredients to Reserve:

- 0.5 oz fresh parmesan, shredded (1/4 protein), for sprinkles
- oil spray

Ingredient for Topping:

- 1 TBSP sour cream (full fat) (optional)

Instructions:

1. Grate zucchini and squeeze out all liquid. I just used a paper towel to squeeze out the liquid, so I wouldn't have to clean my nut milk bag.
2. Heat mini waffle maker. Make sure you place a plate underneath to catch mess.
3. Mix Chaffle ingredients and divide in half.
4. Spray waffle maker on BOTH sides. Zucchini is prone to sticking. Put sprinkles of parmesan at bottom of waffle maker to help make it crispy and on top of mix. Cook 1/2 of Chaffle mix. Remove Chaffle and follow the same instructions for the second Chaffle. Do NOT peek! Wait until all steam is gone.
5. While second Chaffle is cooking, prepare the topping.
6. Place crispy side down on plate and serve with topping.

Note: Serve with 3.5 oz veggie and 6 oz fruit at lunch or 11.5 oz veggie at dinner.

Tuna Melt

Makes 2 lunch or dinner Chaffles in mini waffle maker. These are open faced tuna melts. Provides complete protein and complete fat.

Ingredients for Chaffles:

- 1 large egg, beaten (1/2 protein)
- 0.5 oz shredded parmesan cheese (1/4 fat)
- 1/2 tsp onion powder
- 1/2 tsp garlic powder
- 1/8 tsp seasoned sea salt
- dash dried dill weed
- dash dried parsley

Ingredients to Reserve:

- 0.5 oz fresh parmesan, shredded (1/4 fat), for sprinkles
- oil spray

Ingredients for Topping:

- 2 oz canned tuna (1/2 protein) seasoned with seasoned sea salt and garlic powder
- 0.5 oz Swiss cheese slice (1/2 fat)

Instructions:

1. Heat mini waffle maker. Make sure you place a plate underneath to catch mess.
2. Make Chaffle mix. You will use half of the mix for each Chaffle.
3. Spray waffle maker on top side. Put sprinkles of parmesan at bottom of waffle maker to help make it crispy. Cook 1/2 of Chaffle mix. Remove Chaffle and follow the same instructions for the second Chaffle. Do NOT peek! Wait until all steam is gone.
4. I cooked each Chaffle for 3 minutes. This is a good time to open the can of tuna, drain, weigh 2 oz of tuna and 1 oz of Swiss cheese.
5. Place the crispy side face down into air fryer and put tuna on the softer side. Add 0.25 oz Swiss cheese to each Chaffle. Cook at 360 degrees for 5 minutes, or until cheese is melted. If you don't have an air fryer, cook in oven using broiler.
6. Sprinkle with dill weed.

Notes:

1. I initially tried this with the tuna IN the Chaffle mix and did not like it for this recipe.
2. Serve with 6 oz veggie and 6 oz fruit at lunch or 14 oz veggie at dinner.

Our daughter, Merissa, loves avocado toast and not only does she make it at home she also tries different versions in restaurants. Since she's the expert, I asked her exactly what I should put in this Chaffle and she was spot on. Of course, her avocado is normally on top of toast, but this way works well for Chaffles. It's super yummy!

Merissa's Avocado Toast Chaffles

Makes 2 lunch or dinner Chaffles in mini waffle maker. Provides complete protein and complete fat.

Ingredients for Chaffles:

- 1 large egg, beaten (1/2 protein)
- 0.5 oz unflavored goat cheese, mashed (1/4 protein)
- 1/2 tsp garlic powder
- 1/2 tsp onion powder
- 1/8 tsp seasoned sea salt

Ingredients to Reserve:

- 0.5 oz fresh parmesan, shredded (1/4 protein), for sprinkles
- 2 oz avocado thinly sliced (1 fat) The very small kind is just right.

Ingredient for Topping:

- crushed red pepper (optional)

Instructions:

1. Heat mini waffle maker. Make sure you place a plate underneath to catch mess.
2. Mix the egg and goat cheese together well. Add seasonings.
3. Cut thin slices of avocado amounting to 2 oz. You will use 1 oz of avocado slices per Chaffle.
4. Put 1/4 of parmesan sprinkles at bottom of waffle maker to help make Chaffle crispy. Add 1/2 mix.
5. Place 1 oz of avocado slices sideways onto the mix. Sprinkle some parmesan on top of avocado. Cook Chaffle.
6. Remove Chaffle and follow the same instructions for the second Chaffle. Do NOT peek! Wait until all steam is gone.
7. Let cool on a cooling rack for 1-2 minutes, so Chaffles will be extra crispy and toast like.
8. Top with crushed red pepper.

Note: Serve with 6 oz veggie and 6 oz fruit at lunch or 14 oz veggie at dinner.

Tastes like quiche!

Boursin Arugula Chaffles

Makes 2 lunch or dinner Chaffles in mini waffle maker. Provides complete protein and complete fat. This recipe won't work in a large waffle maker.

Ingredients for Chaffles:

- 1 oz BOURSIN® cheese (1 fat)

Note: BOURSIN® is from France but found at most stores in the US.

- 1 large egg, beaten (1/2 protein)
- 1/2 tsp garlic powder
- 1/2 tsp onion powder
- 1/8 tsp seasoned sea salt

Ingredients to Reserve:

- 1 oz mozzarella cheese, shredded (1/2 protein), for sprinkles
- 0.4 oz fresh arugula, with long stems removed
- oil spray

Instructions:

1. Heat mini waffle maker. Make sure you place a plate underneath to catch mess.
2. Mix Chaffle ingredients together well.

Note: Do not add arugula to mix. Put half arugula on top of each Chaffle mix before closing waffle maker.

3. Spray waffle maker on top and put sprinkles of mozzarella at bottom of waffle maker to help make it crispy.
4. Cook 1/2 of Chaffle mix, adding **half of arugula to top** of mix. Remove Chaffle and follow the same instructions for the second Chaffle. Do NOT peek! Wait until all steam is gone.
5. I cooked each Chaffle for 3 minutes. Place the crispy side face down onto plate.

Notes:

1. For lunch, this pairs nicely with fresh pear and blackberries.
2. Serve with 6 oz veggie and 6 oz fruit at lunch or 14 oz veggie at dinner.

Nicole's Basic Chaffle made into a hamburger. It was for my hubs since I'm a pescatarian. He loved it! Served with air fried parsnips and carrot fries.

Hamburger*

Makes 2 lunch or dinner Chaffles in mini waffle maker. Would not work in a large waffle maker. Provides complete protein, complete fat, and 3 oz veggies.

Ingredients for Chaffles:

- 1 large egg, beaten (1/2 protein)
- 0.5 oz mozzarella or cheddar cheese, shredded (1/2 fat)
- 1/2 tsp onion powder
- 1/2 tsp garlic powder
- dash of sea salt

Ingredients to Reserve:

- 0.5 oz mozzarella or cheddar cheese, shredded (1/2 fat), for sprinkles
- oil spray

Ingredients for Sandwich (Hamburger):

- 2 oz cooked ground beef, or ground turkey (1/2 protein)
- 3 oz raw mix of sliced tomato and lettuce (3 oz veggie)
- pinch of seasoned sea salt to season meat
- sugar free ketchup (free condiment)
- yellow mustard (free condiment)

Note: I mixed the ketchup with the mustard.

Instructions:

1. Heat mini waffle maker. Place a plate underneath to catch the mess.
2. Shape the hamburger patty the size of the mini waffle maker and make it very thin. Season with seasoned sea salt. It will be about 3 oz raw for beef. Set aside.
3. Prepare veggies.
4. Cook hamburger patty in a pan sprayed with oil.
5. Spray waffle maker. Sprinkle 1/2 of reserved cheese onto bottom of waffle maker. Add half Chaffle mix. Remove Chaffle, spray waffle maker, and follow the same instructions for the second Chaffle.
6. Assemble hamburger (sandwich): start with first Chaffle, add hamburger patty, add condiment (put condiment onto meat), add veggies, then add second Chaffle. Do not put sauce directly onto the Chaffle or it will get soggy.

Note: Serve with 3 oz veggie and 6 oz fruit for a complete lunch or serve with 11 ounces veggies for a complete dinner.

I've never in my life made a Philly Cheesesteak, nor have I ever eaten one. It was through a conversation with my son that I thought of this. I'm not sure if this is like a true Philly Cheesesteak, but I know that the hubs loved it!

Philly Cheesesteak

Makes 2 lunch or dinner Chaffles in mini waffle maker. Would not work in a large waffle maker. Provides complete protein, complete fat, and 3 oz veggies.

Ingredients for Chaffles:

- 1 large egg, beaten (1/2 protein)
- 0.5 oz mozzarella cheese, shredded (1/2 fat)
- 1/2 tsp onion powder
- 1/2 tsp garlic powder
- dash of sea salt

Ingredients to Reserve:

- 0.5 oz mozzarella cheese, shredded (1/2 fat), for sprinkles
- oil spray

Ingredients for Sandwich (Cheesesteak):

- 4 oz raw mix of sliced onion and sliced green bell pepper, makes 3 oz cooked. Sauté in oil spray until browned (3 oz veggie)
- 2 oz raw thinly sliced beef, makes 1 oz cooked (1/4 protein)
- pinch of seasoned sea salt to season meat
- 0.5 oz sliced provolone cheese (1/4 protein)

Instructions:

1. Heat mini waffle maker. Place plate underneath to catch any mess.
2. Sauté onion and bell pepper in pan sprayed with oil. Once veggies are browned remove from heat.
3. Spray waffle maker and cook steak, seasoned with seasoned sea salt, in your mini waffle maker. Flip steak to cook other side. Don't overcook, it will cook fast! Remove steak and put aside in pan with veggies.
4. Spray mini waffle maker with oil. No need to remove juice from beef unless beef has lots of fat.
5. Sprinkle 1/2 of reserved cheese onto bottom of waffle maker. Add half Chaffle mix. Remove Chaffle, spray waffle maker, and follow the same instructions for the second Chaffle.
6. Assemble sandwich: start with the first Chaffle, add beef, add veggies, add provolone cheese, then add the second Chaffle.
7. Put entire sandwich into waffle maker and squeeze down to heat up sandwich and melt the cheese. Use potholder to press down.

Note: Serve with 3 oz veggie and 6 oz fruit for a complete lunch or serve with 11 ounces veggies for a complete dinner.

This was amazing and so easy! I experimented again and my husband got to help me eat the Chaffles. We loved this one!

Broccoli & Cheese Chaffles*

Makes 2 lunch or dinner Chaffles in mini waffle maker. This would work in a large waffle maker. Provides full protein, fat, and 2 oz veggies.

Ingredients for Chaffles:

- 1 large egg, beaten (1/2 protein)
- 1 oz cheddar cheese, shredded (1/2 protein)
- 2 oz cooked broccoli florets, no stems
- 1/4 tsp garlic granules
- pinch of seasoned sea salt, to season broccoli

Ingredient to Reserve:

- 1 oz cheddar cheese, shredded (1 fat), for sprinkles divided into fourths

Instructions:

1. Steam broccoli in microwave with some water. Drain well.
2. Season broccoli with seasoned sea salt.
3. Heat mini waffle maker. Place a plate underneath to catch the mess.
4. Mix Chaffle ingredients.
5. No need to spray any oil on waffle maker for this recipe, if using a quality waffle maker.
6. Put 1/4 cheese sprinkles on bottom of waffle maker. This helps make it crispy. Add half the mix. Put 1/4 cheese sprinkles on top of mix.
7. Cook until steam is gone. Repeat the same instructions with the second Chaffle. Cook longer to make it crispier.
8. Cool on a wire cooling rack for 1-2 minutes, so it's crispier.

Note: Serve with 4 oz veggies and 6 oz fruit at lunch or 12 oz veggies at dinner.

Taco Chaffles*

Makes 2 lunch or dinner Chaffles in mini waffle maker. This provides complete protein and fat.

Ingredients for Chaffles:

- 1 large egg, beaten (1/2 protein)
- 1.5 oz cooked ground beef (or ground turkey) (3/8 protein)
- 0.25 oz cheddar cheese, shredded (1/8 protein)
- 1/2 tsp baking powder
- 1/2 tsp onion powder
- 3/4 tsp taco seasoning
- 1/4 tsp salt

Note: My family tried this with 2 oz beef, and everyone said it was too meaty and liked this version with 1.5 oz beef the best. The leaner the meat, the more seasoning you will need. I used 85% lean, grass-fed ground beef.

Ingredients to Reserve:

- 1 oz cheddar cheese, shredded (full fat), for sprinkles and divided into fourths
- oil spray

Ingredient for Topping:

- salsa (optional)

Instructions:

1. Spray a pan with oil and cook the meat with taco seasoning.
2. Heat mini waffle maker. Place a plate underneath to catch the mess.
3. Mix all Chaffle ingredients together. Divide mix in half.
4. No need to spray any oil on waffle maker for this recipe, if using quality waffle maker product.
5. Put cheese sprinkles on bottom of waffle maker and add half mix. Put cheese sprinkles on top of mix. Cook until all steam is gone. Repeat the same instructions with the second Chaffle. The longer you cook it, the crispier it gets.

Notes:

1. Can be made ahead of time. Works reheated in toaster or air fryer. Can freeze.
2. Serve with 6 oz veggie and 6 oz fruit for a complete lunch or serve with 14 ounces veggies for a complete dinner.

I made this for my husband. His eyes got big when he tasted it and he said, "Wow! This is delicious!"

Chicken Parmesan Chaffles*

Makes 2 lunch or dinner Chaffles in mini waffle maker. Provides full protein and fat.

Ingredients for Chaffles:

- 1 large egg, beaten (1/2 protein)
- 2 oz cooked chicken breast shredded (1/2 protein) I used canned chicken breast.
- 0.5 oz mozzarella cheese, shredded (1/2 fat)
- 1/4 tsp Italian Seasoning
- 1/2 tsp garlic granules

Ingredients to Reserve:

- 0.5 oz fresh parmesan cheese, shredded (1/2 fat), for sprinkles
- olive oil spray

Ingredient for Topping:

- 2 oz RAO'S HOMEMADE® Marinara Sauce (free condiment)

Instructions:

1. Heat mini waffle maker. Place a plate underneath to catch the mess.
2. Mix Chaffle ingredients and divide in half.
3. Spray top of waffle maker.
4. Put half of cheese sprinkles on bottom of waffle maker. Put half mixture into waffle maker and cook until steam is gone. Follow the same instructions to cook the second Chaffle.
5. Top with *heated* marinara sauce.

Note: Serve with 6 oz veggie and 6 oz fruit for a complete lunch or serve with 14 ounces veggies for a complete dinner.

I made both tuna and chicken and had my family taste the chicken, since I don't eat meat. They loved both. We did a "Chaffle Tapas" today, so I could get family to try several different kinds. Chaffles are not only yummy, but so much fun!

Buffalo Tuna (or Chicken) Chaffles

Makes 2 lunch or dinner Chaffles in mini waffle maker. Provides complete protein and fat.

Ingredients for Chaffles:

- 2 oz tuna, or 2 oz cooked chicken, shredded (1/2 protein)
- 1 large egg, beaten (1/2 protein)
- 0.5 oz cheddar cheese, shredded (1/2 fat)
- 1/2 tsp baking powder
- 1 1/2 TBSP FRANK'S REDHOT®WINGS Hot Buffalo Sauce, or 2 TBSP if you want it spicy.

Ingredients to Reserve:

- 0.5 oz cheddar cheese, shredded (1/2 fat), for sprinkles
- oil spray

Instructions:

1. Heat mini waffle maker. Place a plate underneath to catch the mess.
2. Mix all Chaffle ingredients together and divide in half.
3. Spray oil on top of waffle maker. Put half of cheese sprinkles onto the bottom of waffle maker. Put half mix into waffle maker. Cook until steam is gone. Repeat the same instructions with the second Chaffle. The longer you cook it, the crispier it gets.
4. Cook for 3-4 minutes.

Notes:

1. Can be made ahead of time. Can freeze. Works reheated in toaster oven or air fryer.
2. Serve with 6 oz veggies and 6 fruit for a complete lunch, or 14 oz veggies at dinner.

Wow! This new Chaffle creation of mine turned out amazing! I thought of it on New Year's Eve and finally made it. It's great for a special occasion, or anytime you're in the mood for smoked salmon.

Smoked Salmon Chaffles

Makes 2 lunch or dinner Chaffles with mini waffle maker. Provides complete protein, complete fat, and 1/2 oz veggies.

Ingredients for Chaffles:

- 1 large egg, beaten (1/2 protein)
- 2 oz smoked salmon (1/2 protein)
- 0.5 oz mozzarella cheese, shredded (1/2 fat)
- 15 capers (free condiment) These are salty, so omit adding salt.
- 1/2 tsp onion powder

Ingredient to Reserve:

- oil spray

Ingredients for Topping:

- 1/2 oz cream cheese (1/2 fat), Whipped cream cheese is easier.
- 1/2 oz red onion, cut into tiny pieces
- 20 capers (free condiment up to 2 oz.) Capers weigh practically nothing! I used about 10 capers on top of each Chaffle.

Instructions:

1. Cut smoked salmon into small pieces. Dice red onion into tiny pieces.
2. Heat mini waffle maker. Place plate underneath to catch any mess.
3. Mix salmon with one already beaten egg, mozzarella, seasoning, and capers.
4. Spray oil onto both sides of waffle maker.
5. Put HALF of the mix onto waffler maker. Cook until steam is gone. Cook longer to make it crispier. Repeat for the second Chaffle.

Note: No cheese sprinkles for this recipe.

6. I heated up my cream cheese for 10 seconds in microwave so I could spread it easier. Watch out- it sometimes pops! Easier to use whipped cream cheese.
7. Put half cream cheese and half red onions on each Chaffle. Put 10-12 capers on each Chaffle.

Note: Serve with 5.5 oz veggies and 6 oz fruit at lunch or 13.5 oz veggies at dinner.

Who doesn't like mini pizzas? These are easy and fun for the whole family!

Mini Pizza Chaffles*

Makes 2 lunch or dinner mini pizza Chaffles in mini waffle maker. Won't work in a large waffle maker. Provides complete protein and fat.

Ingredients for Chaffle:

- 1 large egg, beaten (1/2 protein)
- 0.5 oz mozzarella cheese, shredded (1/2 fat)
- 1/2 tsp garlic granules or garlic powder
- 1/8 tsp seasoned sea salt

Ingredients to Reserve:

- 0.5 oz mozzarella cheese, shredded (1/2 fat), for sprinkles
- oil spray

Ingredients for Topping:

- 1 oz RAO'S HOMEMADE® Marinara Sauce. Half for each Chaffle. (Free condiment)
- 0.5 oz turkey pepperoni, about 5 pieces each Chaffle. (1/4 protein)
- 0.5 oz mozzarella cheese, shredded (1/4 protein)

Chaffle Instructions:

1. Heat mini waffle maker. Make sure and have a plate underneath to catch mess.
2. Mix Chaffle ingredients. Spray top of waffle maker. Sprinkle half of cheese sprinkles on bottom of waffle maker to help make it crispy. Cook half Chaffle mix. Remove Chaffle. Repeat the same instructions for the second Chaffle.

Topping Instructions:

1. Put crispy side down. Put 1/2 marinara on non-crispy side for each Chaffle. Put pepperoni, then top with the remaining cheese.
2. Cook at 390 degrees in air fryer for 5-6 minutes or put under broiler in the oven.

Note: Serve with 6 oz veggie and 6 oz fruit for a complete lunch or serve with 14 ounces veggies for a complete dinner.

Turkey Bacon Club Sandwich*

Makes 2 lunch or dinner Chaffles in mini waffle maker. Provides complete protein and complete fat. Not recommended in a large waffle maker.

Ingredients for Chaffles:

- 1 large egg, beaten (1/2 protein)
- 0.5 oz cheddar cheese, shredded (1/2 fat)
- 3/4 tsp Everything but the Bagel Seasoning

Ingredients to Reserve:

- 0.5 oz cheddar cheese, shredded (1/2 fat), for sprinkles
- oil spray

Ingredients for Sandwich Filling:

- 0.5 oz turkey bacon cooked in mini waffle maker (1/8 protein)
- 0.5 oz turkey deli heated in mini waffle maker (1/8 protein)
- 0.5 oz slice (approximately) of cheddar cheese (1/4 protein)
- yellow mustard (free condiment)

Instructions:

1. Heat mini waffle maker. Make sure you place a plate underneath to catch mess.
2. Cut turkey bacon in half and cook both pieces in mini waffle maker. Remove cooked turkey bacon. Put turkey deli meat onto mini waffle maker to heat up. Remove turkey deli meat.
3. Spray top of waffle maker. (You don't need to spray the bottom since you will be putting sprinkles of cheese). Put sprinkles of cheddar at bottom of waffle maker to help make it crispy. Cook half of Chaffle mix. Remove Chaffle, spray top of waffle maker, and cook other half of mix. Cook for 3 minutes each. Put Chaffles on wire cooling rack.
4. Put slice of cheddar cheese in between turkey deli and turkey bacon and put in mini waffle maker to heat.
5. Remove bacon, deli, and cheese from waffle maker. Spread yellow mustard onto the turkey deli and assemble sandwich.
6. Do not put mustard directly onto Chaffle or it could get soggy.

Note: Serve with 6 oz veggies and 1 fruit for a complete lunch or serve with 11 ounces veggies for a complete dinner.

I did one Chaffle with pickled jalapeños and one Chaffle with fresh, deseeded, and sliced jalapeños. The first Chaffle in the pic has the fresh jalapeños and the other Chaffle has the pickled ones, and both are yummy!

Jalapeño Cheddar Bread Chaffles

Makes 2 lunch or dinner Chaffles in mini waffle maker. This is my basic Chaffle recipe with cheddar instead of mozzarella and no salt with the pickled jalapeños. I was thinking this would be a good Chaffle for a hamburger, grilled cheese sandwich, etc. Provides half protein and complete fat.

Ingredients for Chaffles:

- 1 large egg, beaten (1/2 protein)
- 0.5 oz cheddar cheese, shredded (1/2 fat)
- 1/2 tsp garlic powder
- 1/2 tsp onion powder
- No salt if using pickled jalapeños.
- If using fresh jalapeños, add a dash of salt.

Ingredients to Reserve:

- 0.5 oz cheddar cheese, shredded (1/2 fat), for sprinkles
- 5 slices of jalapeños, either use pickled, sliced jalapeños or fresh sliced (free condiment)
- oil spray

Instructions:

1. Heat mini waffle maker. Make sure you place a plate underneath to catch mess.
2. Mix all Chaffle ingredients together. Divide in half.
3. Spray waffle maker on top side. Put sprinkles of cheddar at bottom of waffle maker to help make it crispy. Add 1/2 of Chaffle mix and place 5 sliced jalapeños on mix. Cook Chaffle mix. Remove Chaffle and follow the same instructions for the second Chaffle. Do NOT peek! Wait until all steam is gone.
4. Cook each Chaffle for 3 minutes, or longer, if you want it crispier.
5. Cool them 1-2 minutes on a wire cooling rack.

Notes:

1. For a sandwich: add 2 oz protein for a sandwich filling and count the cheese in the Chaffle as a fat.
2. At lunch serve with 6 oz veggies and 6 oz fruit, or at dinner with 14 oz veggies.

It's been a long time since I've had a grilled cheese sandwich and now the wait is over! It was so yummy! This would pair well with soup!

Grilled Cheese Sandwich Chaffles*

Makes 2 lunch or dinner Chaffles in mini waffle maker. Provides complete protein and complete fat. Not recommended in a large waffle maker.

Ingredients for Chaffles:

- 1 large egg, beaten (1/2 protein)
- 0.5 oz cheddar cheese, shredded (1/2 fat)
- 3/4 tsp "Everything but the Bagel Seasoning"

Ingredients to Reserve:

- 0.5 oz cheddar cheese, shredded (1/2 fat), for sprinkles
- oil spray

Ingredient for Sandwich Filling:

- 1 oz of cheddar cheese slice (1/2 protein)

Instructions:

1. Heat mini waffle maker. Make sure you place a plate underneath to catch mess.
2. Spray top of waffle maker. You don't need to spray the bottom since you will be putting sprinkles of cheese. Put sprinkles of cheddar at bottom of waffle maker to help make it crispy. Cook half Chaffle mix. Remove Chaffle and follow the same instructions for the second Chaffle. Cook each Chaffle for 3 minutes.
3. Put crispy side of Chaffle onto plate. Place slice of cheddar cheese on top of Chaffle and cover with the other Chaffle.
4. Make sure crispy part is facing out. Put entire sandwich back into the mini waffle maker to melt cheese. Press on waffle maker, being careful not to burn yourself. I used a potholder to press. Once cheese is melted, slice sandwich in half and serve.

Note: Serve with 6 oz veggies and 1 fruit for a complete lunch or serve with 11 ounces veggies for a complete dinner.

Do any of you miss going to seafood restaurants? Well, look no further! This creation was absolutely delicious! I was truly amazed that it really tasted like a crab cake!

Crab Cake Chaffles

Makes 2 lunch or dinner Chaffles in mini waffle maker. Provides complete protein and complete fat. Should work in a large waffle maker.

Ingredients for Chaffles:

- 1 large egg, beaten (1/2 protein)
- 0.25 oz mozzarella cheese shredded (1/4 fat)- not much cheese.
- 2 oz fresh crab, pulled apart/shredded by hand (1/2 protein)
- pinch garlic powder
- pinch onion powder
- 1/4 tsp butter extract
- 1/2 tsp Dijon mustard
- 1/4 tsp BRAGG® Liquid Aminos (or GF soy sauce)
- 1/2 TBSP mayo or 0.25 oz (1/2 fat)
- 1/2 tsp OLD BAY® Seasoning (near seafood department at grocery)
- 1/2 TBSP fresh (or dried parsley) Free condiment. No weight.

Ingredients to Reserve:

- 0.25 oz mozzarella cheese, shredded (1/4 fat), for sprinkles
- oil spray

Ingredients for Topping:

- fresh lemon to squeeze (optional)
- fresh parsley, cut (optional)

Instructions:

1. Heat mini waffle maker. Make sure you place a plate underneath to catch mess.
2. Mix all Chaffle ingredients. Divide mix in half.
3. Spray top AND bottom of waffle maker since there is not much cheese. Put half of cheese sprinkles at bottom of waffle maker to help make it crispy. Cook half of Chaffle mix. Follow the same instructions for the second Chaffle.
4. Serve Chaffles with fresh parsley on top and squeezed lemon.

Notes:

1. I also tried them with TABASCO® and with Tartar sauce. They were best plain or with squeezed lemon.
2. Pairs well with corn on the cob!
3. At lunch serve with 6 oz veggies and 6 oz fruit, or at dinner with 14 oz veggies.

These were so crispy, crunchy, and yummy! The texture is fabulous! I bet the whole family will want them!

Corn Fritters Chaffles

Makes 3 lunch or dinner Chaffles in the mini waffle maker or in a large waffle maker. Provides full protein, 3 oz veggies, and 1/2 fat.

Ingredients for Chaffles:

- 3 oz frozen corn, defrosted (1/2 veggie)
- 1 large egg, beaten (1/2 protein)
- 0.5 oz cheddar cheese, shredded (1/4 protein)
- 1/2 tsp onion powder
- 1/2 tsp garlic powder
- 1/8 tsp seasoned sea salt
- 1 TBSP, 0.20 oz, fresh green onions, chopped (green part only, free condiment)

Ingredients to Reserve:

- 0.5 oz cheddar cheese, shredded (1/4 protein), sprinkles
- oil spray

Ingredients for Topping:

- 1 TBSP sour cream (1/2 fat)
- 1 TBSP green onion, chopped (free condiment)

Instructions:

1. Heat mini waffle maker. Make sure you place a plate underneath to catch mess.
2. Add other ingredients to corn and green onion. Mix well. Divide mix into thirds.
3. Spray waffle maker on the top. Put sprinkles of cheddar at bottom of waffle maker to help make it crispy. Cook 1/3 of Chaffle mix. Remove Chaffle and follow the same instructions for the second and third Chaffles. Do NOT peek! Wait until all steam is gone.
4. I cooked each Chaffle for 3 minutes. This is a good time to prepare the topping.
5. Place the crispy side face down onto plate and put topping on the softer side.

Notes:

1. For a complete meal, add 3 oz veggies, 1/2 fat, and 6 oz fruit for lunch. Add 11 oz veggies and 1/2 fat for dinner.
2. These would freeze and toast well.

Cauliflower Rice Pizza Chaffles

Makes 4 dinner Chaffles in the mini waffle maker. Provides complete protein, fat, and 7 oz veggies. Will not work in a large waffle maker. It will either stick or fall apart.

Ingredients for Chaffles:

- One 12 oz bag frozen cauliflower rice. Shrinks to 7 oz. once defrosted and the water is squeezed out.

Note: WHOLE FOODS® frozen cauliflower rice is best, since it gets crispy!

- 1 large egg, beaten (1/2 protein)
- 0.5 oz fresh parmesan cheese shredded (1/2 fat) This helps to make it firm and crispy.
- 1 tsp Italian seasoning
- 1/2 tsp garlic powder
- 1/8 tsp seasoned sea salt

Ingredients to Reserve:

- 0.5 oz fresh parmesan cheese, shredded (1/2 fat), for sprinkles
- oil spray
- fresh basil

Ingredients for Topping:

- 2 ounces of RAO'S HOMEMADE® Marinara Sauce (free condiment), mixed with optional garlic, and spread thinly on top of cooked cauliflower crust.
- 1 oz mozzarella cheese, shredded (1/2 protein)
- 1 garlic clove, minced (optional)

Instructions:

1. Heat mini waffle maker. Make sure you place a plate underneath to catch mess.
2. Use a nut milk bag or cheesecloth and squeeze out excess water after you defrost the cauliflower rice. You cannot skip this step, or you will have mushy Chaffles that stick. You want firm and crispy pizza Chaffles.
3. Mix all Chaffle ingredients. Divide mix into fourths.
4. Spray top and bottom of waffle maker. Cauliflower can stick! Put sprinkles of parmesan at bottom of waffle maker to help make it crispy. Cook 1/4 Chaffle mix. Do NOT peek! Remove Chaffle and repeat instructions for second, third, and fourth Chaffles.
5. While Chaffles are cooking, chiffonnade the basil.
6. Cook each Chaffle for 5 minutes and cool for 1-2 minutes on a wire cooling rack.
7. Place pizza with crispy side down. Top with sauce, cheese, & garlic.
8. Cook in air fryer 4-5 minutes at 360 degrees. Check at 3 minutes. Once cheese is very melted and pizza appears crunchy, remove and top with fresh basil.

Spinach Artichoke Dip Chaffles

Makes 2 lunch or dinner Chaffles in mini waffle maker. Provides complete protein, complete fat, and 1.3 oz veggies.

Ingredients for Chaffles:

- 1 large egg, beaten (1/2 protein)
- 1 oz artichoke hearts, patted dry and chopped
- 1/2 TBSP mayonnaise (1/2 fat)
- 0.5 oz fresh parmesan cheese, shredded (1/4 protein)
- 1/2 tsp garlic granules
- 1/2 tsp onion powder
- 1/8 tsp seasoned sea salt

Ingredients to Reserve:

- 0.5 oz fresh shredded parmesan cheese (1/4 protein) for sprinkles
- 0.3 oz fresh, baby spinach leaves, outer stems removed
- oil spray

Ingredients for Topping:

- 1/2 TBSP sour cream (1/2 fat)
- dash of dried parsley on top of sour cream

Instructions:

1. Chop artichoke hearts and pat dry.
2. Take off outer stems of baby spinach (reserve).
3. Heat mini waffle maker. Make sure you place a plate underneath to catch mess.
4. Mix all Chaffle ingredients. Spray top of waffle maker. Sprinkle bottom of mini waffle maker with parmesan. Pour 1/2 mix into waffle maker and place 1/2 baby spinach leaves on top. Remove Chaffle once cooked and follow the same instructions for the second Chaffle. Do NOT peek! Wait until all steam is gone. Spinach is prone to sticking.
5. Place crispy side face down on a wire cooling rack for 1-2 minutes.
6. Put topping on each Chaffle.

Note: At lunch serve with 4.7 oz veggies and 6 oz fruit, or at dinner with 12.7 oz veggies.

I was at a store where they had a huge pile of SWEET onions and I had the idea to create this new Chaffle. So, I decided to make something resembling one of my favorites in France. They turned out to be absolutely delicious! I served them at dinner with butternut squash soup and salad.

French Onion Tarte Chaffles

Makes 2 lunch or dinner Chaffles in mini waffle maker. Provides complete protein and 1.5 oz veggies.

Ingredients for Chaffles:

- 1 large egg, beaten (1/2 protein)
- 1.5 oz SWEET onion, diced into small pieces
- 0.5 oz shredded mozzarella cheese (1/4 protein)
- 1/2 tsp onion powder
- 1/2 tsp garlic powder
- 1/8 tsp seasoned sea salt

Ingredient to Reserve:

- 0.5 oz sliced Swiss cheese (1/4 protein). It's usually one slice. Use half for bottom of each Chaffle to make them crispy.

Instructions:

1. Cut onion into small pieces and leave raw.
2. Heat mini waffle maker. Make sure you place a plate underneath to catch any mess.
3. Mix all Chaffle ingredients. Divide mix in half.
4. You don't need to spray waffle maker since you will be putting half a slice of Swiss cheese at bottom of waffle maker to make it crispy, and it will remove easily. If you don't have a good quality mini waffle maker brand, then I encourage you to use oil spray.
5. Cook half Chaffle mix. Remove Chaffle and follow the same instructions for the second Chaffle.

Notes:

1. Shredded Swiss cheese would work well, but I have not seen it at the store, and I don't want to spend time grating it.
2. Great served with soup or salad.
3. Add 4.5 oz veggies, 1 fat, and 6 oz fruit for a complete lunch or 12.5 oz veggies and 1 fat for a complete dinner.
4. You could count both cheeses as a fat and add 2 oz protein to your lunch or dinner.

My husband was super happy about this new creation of mine and said it was really yummy! Not surprised he liked the turkey bacon, but surprised he liked the jalapeños!

Turkey Bacon Jalapeño Popper Chaffles

Makes 2 lunch or dinner Chaffles in mini waffle maker or in a large waffle maker. Provides 5/8 protein and complete fat.

Ingredients for Chaffles:

- 1 large egg, beaten (1/2 protein)
- 0.5 oz cheddar cheese, shredded (1/2 fat)
- 0.5 oz precooked turkey bacon cut into small pieces (1/8 protein)
- 10 slices of pickled jalapeño- 5 for each of the two Chaffles (free condiment)
- 1/2 tsp onion powder
- 1/2 garlic powder
- NO salt!

Ingredients to Reserve:

- 0.5 oz cheddar cheese, shredded (1/2 fat), for sprinkles
- oil spray

Instructions:

1. Cook the turkey bacon. It's about 3-4 slices.
2. Place 10 pickled jalapeños on paper towel to remove some of the moisture, or your Chaffle won't be as crispy.
3. Heat mini waffle maker. Make sure you place a plate underneath to catch mess.
4. Spray waffle maker on top and put sprinkles of cheddar at bottom of waffle maker to help make it crispy. Cook 1/2 of Chaffle mix. Remove Chaffle and follow the same instructions for the second Chaffle. Do NOT peek! Wait until all steam is gone.
5. I cooked each Chaffle for 4 minutes.

Note: For lunch serve with 1.5 oz protein, 6 oz veggies, and 6 oz fruit. No more fat. For dinner serve with 1.5 oz protein and 14 oz veggies. No more fat.

Olive Bread Chaffles

Makes 2 lunch or dinner Chaffles in mini waffle maker. Provides complete protein and 1/2 fat.

Ingredients for Chaffles:

- 1 large egg, beaten (1/2 protein)
- 0.5 oz fresh parmesan cheese, shredded (1/4 protein)
- 1/2 tsp garlic powder
- 1/2 tsp onion powder
- No salt

Ingredients to Reserve:

- 0.5 oz mozzarella cheese, shredded (1/4 protein)
- 1 oz fresh, whole olives, pitted and sliced (1/2 fat)
- oil spray

Instructions:

1. Heat mini waffle maker. Make sure you place a plate underneath to catch mess.
2. Mix all Chaffle ingredients together. Divide in half.
3. Spray waffle maker on top side. Put sprinkles of mozzarella on bottom of waffle maker to help make it crispy. Add 1/2 of Chaffle mix and place 5 sliced olives on top of mix. Cook Chaffle mix. Remove Chaffle and follow the same instructions for the second Chaffle. Do NOT peek! Wait until all steam is gone.
4. Cook each Chaffle for 3 minutes, or longer, if you want it crispier.
5. Cool Chaffles 1-2 minutes on a wire cooling rack.

Note: Side with 6 oz veggies, 6 oz fruit, 1/2 oz fat for lunch, or 14 oz veggies and 1/2 fat for dinner.

MAINTENANCE

Our son, Alessio, wants my carrot cake every year for his birthday. He loves it! It was a recipe from my mom that I changed over the years. This Chaffle recipe is very close to my own "secret recipe" without the sugar and flour!

Alessio's Carrot Cake Chaffles

Makes 3 breakfast Chaffles in mini waffle maker. Provides complete grain, complete protein, and complete fruit. However, with the addition of a fat, it is for maintenance. I would not recommend a large waffle maker for this recipe unless it's in sections and you can layer the cake.

Ingredients for Chaffles:

- 1 large egg, beaten (1/2 protein)
- 1 oz uncooked oats (full grain)
- 1.5 oz raw carrots, grated
- 2 oz banana, mashed (used as a sweetener)
- 0.5 oz crushed pineapple with ALL juice squeezed out using paper towel
- 0.5 oz mozzarella cheese, shredded (1/4 protein)
- 2 tsp vanilla
- 1 tsp cinnamon
- 1/4 tsp baking powder
- 1/8 tsp baking soda

Ingredients to Reserve:

- 0.5 oz mozzarella (1/4 protein), for sprinkles
- oil spray

Ingredients for Topping:

- 1 oz cream cheese (full fat). It's easier with whipped cream cheese.
- 2 oz crushed pineapple, drained, but don't squeeze out juice
- dash vanilla

Instructions:

1. Peel and grate 1.5 oz carrot. Squeeze juice out from crushed pineapple until it weighs 0.5 oz, using a paper towel.
2. Heat mini waffle maker. Make sure you place a plate underneath to catch mess.
3. Mash banana and add other Chaffle ingredients. (Reserve 0.5 oz mozzarella for sprinkles). Mix well and divide into thirds.
4. Spray waffle maker on both sides. Carrots and pineapple tend to stick. Put sprinkles of mozzarella at bottom of waffle maker to help make it crispy. Cook 1/3 of Chaffle mix. Remove Chaffle and follow the same instructions for the second and third Chaffles. Do NOT peek! Wait until all steam is gone.
5. Make topping while Chaffles are cooking. Add topping ingredients together.
6. Let Chaffles cool for 1-2 minutes on a wire cooling rack before adding topping.
7. Spread topping on each Chaffle and layer them.

Notes: It's NOT recommended to eat refrigerated. I assure you, putting it in the fridge ruins it. I tried. Also, I would not recommend altering this recipe until you try it as written first. FYI, it's the only recipe in this book that I have mentioned this.

Reuben Sandwich

Makes 2 lunch or dinner Chaffles in mini waffle maker. Will not work in a large waffle maker. Provides complete protein, complete fat, 1 oz veggies, and an additional protein serving, so this is for maintenance.

Ingredients for Rye Chaffle Bread:

- 1 large egg, beaten (1/2 protein)
- 1/4 tsp caraway seeds, to give the rye flavor
- 1/4 tsp baking powder
- 1/8 tsp seasoned sea salt
- 1/8 tsp onion powder

Ingredients to Reserve:

- 0.5 oz Swiss cheese, shredded (1/2 fat), for sprinkles
- oil spray

Ingredients for Sandwich Filling:

- 2 oz corned beef (1/2 protein)
- 1 oz Swiss cheese slice (extra protein, hence maintenance)
- 1 oz sauerkraut, drained (optional to add more)

Ingredients for Sauce and Instructions:

Nicole's Thousand Island Dressing

- 1 TBSP sliced dill pickles, finely chopped
- 1 TBSP sweet onion, finely chopped (white onion would work too)
- 1 TBSP mayonnaise, with no added sugar
- 1 tsp ketchup, with no added sugar
- 1/8 tsp seasoned sea salt

Mix together. Makes 2 servings. Use 1/2 portion for sandwich and count as 1/2 fat.

Instructions:

1. Make the Thousand Island Dressing and get the sandwich filling ingredients ready. Mix Chaffle ingredients together.
2. Heat mini waffle maker. Place a plate underneath to catch the mess.
3. Spray top of waffle maker. Sprinkle 1/2 of cheese sprinkles onto bottom of waffle maker. Add half Chaffle mix. Remove Chaffle, spray waffle maker, and follow the same instructions for the second Chaffle.
4. Assemble sandwich. Start with half Chaffle, add meat, Swiss cheese slice, Thousand Island Dressing, and top with sauerkraut. Place second Chaffle on top of sauerkraut. Do not put sauce directly onto the Chaffle or it will get soggy.
5. Put sandwich into air fryer at 360 degrees for 5 minutes or a toaster oven.

Note: Serve with 6 oz veggie and 6 oz fruit for a complete lunch or serve with 13 ounces veggies for a complete dinner.

Not Chaffles, but still...

So simple. So crunchy. So good!

Corn Tortillas

Makes 3 breakfast tortillas in mini waffle maker. Provides full grain and 1/2 protein.

Ingredients for Tortillas:

- 4 oz precooked instant grits (or dry polenta, cooked), adding minimal boiling water to cook.
- 1/2 tsp butter extract
- 1/8 tsp seasoned sea salt
- 1/8 tsp onion powder

Ingredients to Reserve:

- 1 oz Mexican cheese blend (or cheddar cheese), shredded (1/2 protein), for sprinkles

Note: You will use this cheese for sprinkles on both the bottom and top of mix for 3 tortillas, so keep this in mind when you sprinkle the cheese.

- oil spray

Instructions:

1. Let grits cool after cooking. Divide into two 1.5 oz portions and one 1 oz portion.

Note: 1.5 oz best, but we can only have 4 oz grains until maintenance.

2. Flatten each portion by hand to the approximate size of the mini waffle maker.
3. Heat mini waffle maker. Place a plate underneath to catch the mess.
4. Spray oil on top of waffle maker. Put some cheese sprinkles on bottom of waffle maker. Add 1/3 of the mix. Top with more cheese sprinkles. This helps make it crispy. The longer you cook it the crispier it gets!
5. Cook each tortilla for 3 minutes.
6. Repeat the same instructions three times.
7. Cool on wire cooling rack for 1-2 minutes

Note: For breakfast serve with 1/2 protein and 6 oz. fruit.

One of the delicious ways to use my mini waffle maker. Being from Texas, I love Mexican food and have been missing this! It's in the singular form since it's only one egg in case you were wondering.

Huevo Ranchero & Corn Tortillas

Makes 3 breakfast tortillas and one egg in mini waffle maker. Provides full grain and full protein.

Ingredients for Chaffles:

- 4 oz precooked instant grits (or dry polenta, cooked), adding minimal boiling water to cook.
- 1/2 tsp butter extract
- 1/8 tsp seasoned sea salt
- 1/8 tsp onion powder

Ingredients to Reserve:

- 1 oz Mexican cheese blend or cheddar cheese, shredded (1/2 protein), for sprinkles

Note: You will use this cheese for sprinkles on both the bottom and top.

- 1 large egg, (1/2 protein), for LAST step. Do not beat egg.
- oil spray

Ingredient for Topping:

- salsa

Instructions:

1. Let grits cool after cooking. Divide into two 1.5 oz portions and one 1 oz portion.

Note: 1.5 oz best, but we can only have 4 oz grains until maintenance.

2. Flatten each portion by hand to the approximate size of the mini waffle maker.
3. Heat mini waffle maker. Place a plate underneath to catch the mess.
4. Spray oil on top of waffle maker. Put some cheese sprinkles on bottom of waffle maker. Add 1/3 of the mix. Top with more cheese sprinkles. This helps make it crispy. The longer you cook it the crispier it gets!
5. Repeat the same instructions three times. Cook each tortilla for 3 minutes and cool on wire cooling rack for 1-2 minutes.
6. Last step is to spray oil on mini waffle maker and crack open one egg and cook. Be careful because the egg can run off the mini waffle maker faster than you can blink! The first time I did it the egg flew off like a rocket onto the floor. Use a utensil to keep it from running off. Or fry egg in a pan. I like my eggs cooked well, so the waffle maker worked for me, plus I didn't have to dirty a pan.
7. Once egg is cooked, put egg on top of one of the corn tortillas and top with salsa.

Note: Side with 6 oz fruit.

Onion Ring*

Put ½ oz shredded mozzarella cheese in mini waffle maker.
Put ½ oz thinly sliced rings of onions on top.
Add garlic powder.
Cover with ½ oz mozzarella cheese and cook until steam is gone.
Remove with a plastic fork and cool 1-2 minutes.
Count the 1 oz cheese as a fat at lunch or dinner.

Fried Avocado*

Put ½ oz shredded cheddar cheese in mini waffle maker.
Put 1 oz avocado slices on top.
Add sea salt and garlic granules.
Cover with ½ oz shredded cheddar cheese and cook until steam is gone.
Remove with a plastic fork and cool 1-2 minutes.
Count the avocado as ½ fat, the cheese as ½ fat AND ¼ protein at lunch or dinner.

Fried Pickles*

Put ½ oz shredded Mexican style cheese in mini waffle maker.
Put 1 oz sliced pickled chips, rinsed, and patted dry, on top of cheese.
Cover with ½ oz Mexican style cheese and cook until steam is gone.
Remove with a plastic fork and cool 1-2 minutes.
Count the 1 oz cheese as a fat at lunch or dinner.

"Not Deep Fried" Mushrooms*

2 oz fresh, sliced, and cooked mushrooms that have been drained and pressed with paper towel to get moisture out. Season with sea salt while cooking. Spray top of mini waffle maker with oil. Put ½ oz shredded mozzarella cheese in mini waffle maker. Top with cooked mushrooms, pinch garlic granules, and cover with ½ oz mozzarella cheese. Cook until steam is gone. Remove with a plastic fork and let cool for 1-2 minutes. Count cheese as fat and mushrooms as 2 oz veggies for lunch or dinner.

Cheddar Jalapeño Nacho*

Who needs nachos when you can have this?! So delicious! 1 oz shredded cheddar and about 5-6 pickled, sliced jalapeños. Crunchy and tasty! Put ½ oz shredded cheddar on bottom of mini waffle maker. Place 5-6 pickled, sliced jalapeños on top. Put other ½ oz of shredded cheddar on top of jalapeños. Close lid. Cook until steam is gone. Remove carefully with plastic fork. Wait one minute. Count the 1 oz cheese as a fat at lunch or dinner.

HOMEMADE NUT BUTTERS

Peanut Butter

Funny story. I tried to make almond butter one time in my high-powered blender and the almonds turned into a pulverized powder, so I dumped it out. I figured something was wrong with my almonds, or I had messed up and put the speed too high.

Fast forward about 5 years and today I was determined to make peanut butter. Lo and behold, the same thing happened. These were good peanuts too! So, I did what I should have done years ago and looked it up. Apparently, it's normal to turn into powder, but you just keep it on and then the powder becomes a creamy and delicious peanut butter!!!

I used my high-powered blender, but a food processor works best because it is much easier to clean.

I started with 10 oz roasted and lightly salted peanuts, that had already been shelled, and I didn't add anything.

I encourage you to try this!

Pecan Butter

Roast pecan halves in the oven at 375 degrees for 5-8 minutes and let cool slightly. Be careful not to over roast or your pecan butter won't taste good.

Put them in a high-powered blender and initially they turn into a powder, but keep it going and it becomes a creamy pecan butter!

This was my last time to use the high-powered blender to make a nut butter. A food processor works just as well and so much easier to clean.

Hazelnut Butter

As you probably know by now, I love and need variety, but I also get on these kicks with experimenting. I'm just curious! This hazelnut butter might be my favorite! It's seriously amazing!

It's more time consuming than the others, but worth every minute of time. I had a totally failed attempt at making it yesterday. It was like a hazelnut paste. I was in a hurry and decided not to remove all the skins from the nuts and ruined it! It would not get creamy, even if I added lots of oil. The skins also gave the nut butter a bitter aftertaste. The color was off too.

I bought roasted and unsalted hazelnuts. The second time around, I put the nuts in a clean kitchen towel and just kept making friction until the skin was removed. All of it! It's a tedious process, but worth it in the end. Also, I read online that roasting them brings out the oils. So even though they were roasted, I roasted them again for 8 minutes at 375 degrees. This time I used my food processor and it's way easier to clean than my high-powered blender. I didn't think it would work because it's very old, but it worked like a charm. The nuts looked like sand at first, but after 10 minutes I had a creamy, delectable hazelnut butter! I did check it every few minutes.

Almond Butter

Use 12 oz or more raw almonds and roast them at 350 for 8 minutes. Be careful not to overcook or your almond butter will taste burned. Did that! Add almonds to food processor and blend until it forms a pulverized looking powder. Continue to blend stopping periodically to remove nut butter from the sides. Blend until a desired smooth consistency.
Store in a closed container at room temperature for 7-10 days or in the refrigerator for 3 months.

Acknowledgments

A big thank you to:

My husband, Nino, who believed in my Chaffle cookbook from the beginning and cheered me along the way. You enthusiastically looked forward to tasting my new Chaffle creations, and your input was very beneficial in determining which recipes to include. I had so much fun hearing your responses to each new recipe! You gave me support and put a great deal of time into creating my cool logo and other logistics. I appreciate you and I love you!

My grown children, Alessio and Merissa, who helped inspire me to be my best. I am happy you jumped on the Chaffle train and eagerly tried my creations. You have told me for many years that I should write a cookbook, and your belief in me filled me with courage. I love you both so much!

My dad and mom, Ron and Gigi, for always being my biggest fans no matter what I pursued and where I went. You have emboldened me to follow my dreams! I am blessed by you both each and every day, and I love you very much!

My mom, Gigi, who helped me to figure out the best recipe fonts and sizes and went through every single recipe (several times) to check for any mistakes. I am very impressed at your editing skills and could not have done it without your help! You are amazing and I greatly benefitted from your eagle eyes!

My sister, Désirée, who was continually willing to listen to and support me. You also encouraged me in writing blogs and were so sweet in giving feedback. No matter what I do, you are always by my side. Thank you for making my life better by being the best sister!

My Aunt Joan, Aunt Susie, and my cousin, Amber who gave me their crucial feedback for this cookbook. I texted *so* many questions and asked for *so* much feedback from the ladies in my family.

My cousin, Ginger, who spent countless hours helping me with intellectual property legal advice. You very enthusiastically jumped right in and it didn't matter how much time you spent, because your concern was all about helping me. I greatly appreciate you!

My dear friend, Christina Swan, Ph.D. who introduced me to the no sugar, no flour community! This cookbook would not be possible without your love, feedback, wisdom, and encouragement. You even surprised me early on with a preliminary Chaffle cookbook of my recipes that you made for me with the title "Chaffle Mania," so this title is yours!

The no sugar, no flour Facebook community, who labeled me *"The Chaffle Queen"* and who continually motivated me to write a Chaffle Cookbook. Not only did you encourage me, you also sent me the most thoughtful private messages and wrote amazingly encouraging posts and comments on Facebook and Instagram.

Kelly Aul and her sister Natalie, who were very kind and generous in allowing me to share my Facebook page, recipes, and my cookbook release on their Facebook page. Without your support, encouragement, and feedback, this cookbook would not exist. Natalie, you were always very helpful in answering any of my questions, and Kelly, my publisher, you were so very patient, prompt, and professional.

YOU! Thank you for buying this cookbook! I am very appreciative of your support.

INDEX

Z

About the Author

Nicole De Falcis is from Texas and currently lives in Austin, where she graduated from the University of Texas. After graduation, she lived in 3 different European countries and continued to travel the world extensively. While living abroad and traveling, she developed a passion for cooking! She is a pescatarian and loves a variety of cuisines.

Once settled back in the United States, she worked in the corporate world as a sales manager and a corporate trainer. After she married her Swiss-Italian husband and had two wonderful children, she eventually became a teacher for 15 years. In June 2019, she decided to semi-retire from teaching to pursue other ventures.

She loves to spend time with family and friends, travel the world, read, make photo books, and create new recipes.

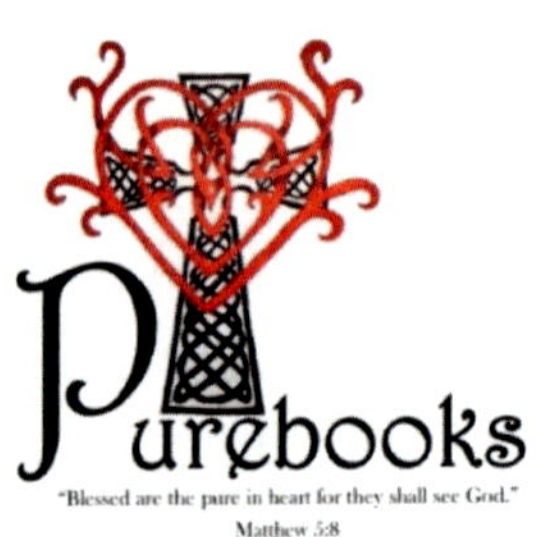

This book was published by Purebooks Publishing Company which is a part of Kelly's Complete Digital Design.

KELLYAULNOVELS.COM

Made in the USA
Las Vegas, NV
11 May 2023